Primary Teaching and the Negotiation of Power

Sylvia M. Warham

Senior Lecturer in Early Years Education
Rolle Faculty of Education,
University of Plymouth

P·C·P
Paul Chapman
Publishing Ltd

Paul Chapman Publishing Ltd
144 Liverpool Road
London
N1 1LA

British Library Cataloguing in Publication Data

Warham, Sylvia
  Primary Teaching and the Negotiation of Power
  I. Title
  371.1
ISBN 1 85396 228 7

Typeset by Inforum, Rowlands Castle, Hants
Printed and bound by Athenaeum Press, Newcastle-upon-Tyne

A B C D E F G H   9 8 7 6 5 4 3

Contents

Introduction   ix

1. A dominant identity: power   1

2. A less dominant identity: power by consent   9

3. Constructively ambiguous identities: the operation of power in the classroom   17

4. Teaching styles: the balance of power   30

5. When teachers use the media: power failure   39

6. What do teachers do beyond their work in the classroom? Power in the staffroom   49

7. Power in the community: teachers and parents   56

8. Influences beyond the classroom that affect a teacher's work: power and leadership   62

9. The influences on teachers' work beyond the school: the wider power context   76

10. Teaching and the negotiation of power   88

Suggested reading   93

References   96

Index   97

For Rod and Giles

Know then thyself, presume not God to scan,
The proper study of mankind is man . . .
Sole judge of truth, in endless error hurled:
The glory, jest and riddle of the world!
(Alexander Pope, *An Essay on Man*)

Introduction

In times of change, when questions are being asked nationally about teaching standards and the most effective methods of training teachers, never has it been more important to ask: How do Primary teachers teach?

There can be little doubt that teaching and learning is a two-way process. For example, no teacher can make a pupil learn. Teaching and learning can only take place with the co-operation of the teacher and the learner. In this sense, teaching and learning are a negotiation because the process requires the consent of both the teacher and the learner, but what is it that they actually negotiate?

After many years of teaching and observing teachers in their classrooms, it seemed to me that teachers and pupils negotiate a power relationship. This power relationship has nothing to do with institutions, or the power and authority of the teacher, or even whether or not the teacher has an authoritarian style of teaching. The power that I observed was simply the power generated between two or more people when they communicate with each other.

This communicative power arises out of the practical necessity of deciding who will 'hold the floor' at any given point in a conversation. It is necessary because if everyone spoke at once, no one would be able to hear anyone else or follow what is happening. For this reason, when we hold conversations, there is a continuous negotiation and renegotiation of who will 'hold the floor'. However, when we observe this process of negotiation in the classroom, it soon becomes clear that it is crucial to the teaching and learning process. It determines how much or how little can be learnt, and it affects the quality of learning that can take place.

This book begins by looking at how different teachers set up different identities with their pupils. It examines the range of dominant and less dominant power strategies used by teachers to manage the learning in the classroom. It attempts to show how pupils may also adopt dominant and less dominant power strategies to limit or facilitate what the teacher can do in the classroom. The process of limiting or facilitating learning possibilities, on the part of both the teacher and pupils, illustrates the two-way nature of power relationships and their crucial importance to teaching and learning.

Nevertheless, it would be a mistake to take the myopic view that 'what a teacher does' is confined to the classroom. In present times of change, teachers increasingly undertake responsibilities which extend far beyond the walls of their classrooms. Increasingly the work of a teacher is affected by a far wider power context than that of the school or local community. This book attempts to expose something of the complex power tapestry against which teachers perform their professional activities.

Chapter 1, 'A dominant identity: power', looks at how a teacher describes what she does in her classroom. This teacher says that she sets up 'constructively ambiguous identities in order to get her work done'. But what does she mean by this? A brief extract of a different teacher dismissing her class at break time provides insights into one of the identities a teacher may adopt: a dominant identity. This teacher assumes a dominant identity by using dominant power strategies with her pupils. The pupils also use dominant strategies with their teacher, and in this way the context for learning is negotiated.

Chapter 2, 'A less dominant identity: power by consent', observes another teacher working in her classroom. It recognises the fact that, during the course of a day, teachers may teach different kinds of lessons. Sometimes teachers stand at the front of the class and teach, at other times teachers talk about 'handing over the learning to the children'. This chapter asks: What happens when the teacher hands over the learning to the children? It examines an example of another teacher holding a discussion with a group of six-year-olds, about how people think. This teacher adopts less dominant power strategies and adopts a less dominant identity.

Chapter 3, 'Constructively ambiguous identities: the operation of power in the classroom', recognises the fact that many teachers operate small group and individual work simultaneously. It asks: What happens to the power relationships then? This chapter illustrates a teacher slipping in rapid succession from one identity to another. She does this because the children are operating power strategies upon her. Here we really begin to see something of the negotiation that is going on between the teacher and pupils. We gain insights into the skills of the teacher in managing the power relationships in the classroom.

Chapter 4, 'Teaching styles: the balance of power', examines two further examples, one of a teacher explaining a maths game to a group and another of a teacher holding a discussion about whether or not fish can feel. This teacher adopts a very dominant position in the discussion and sets up very dominant power strategies. This leads to potentially difficult situations. The children respond to this discussion in a very different manner, leading to confrontations. From this example it is concluded that

- the habitual power relationships set up between teachers and their pupils are one way of describing the different styles with which teachers operate in the classroom;
- teachers have choices about the ways in which they manage the power relationships in their classrooms, but this choice is limited;
- effective teachers understand the limits beyond which they must not go if they are to maintain control of the power relationships in their classrooms; and
- effective teachers are aware of the benefits of both dominant and less dominant power strategies.

Chapter 5, 'When teachers use the media: power failure', examines a radio broadcast for reception class children, and asks how far, and in what senses, can this be described as a teaching activity? It concludes that there is a difference between teaching and instruction and that this difference rests in the teacher's identity and his or her power strategies.

Chapter 6, 'What do teachers do beyond their work in the classroom? Power in the staffroom', recognises the fact that the work of a teacher is not confined to work in the classroom with children. Teachers attend and lead meetings, conferences and in-service courses. This chapter asks: What can we learn about primary teaching by looking at teachers talking to teachers? It examines a meeting between teachers. The conversation illustrates how teachers have to have the ability to synthesise a wide range of issues, ranging from legal requirements to practical and theoretical considerations before they can make their teaching plans. It also highlights the teachers' use of professional language and the teachers' need to be literate in the language in which professional activities are couched. This chapter further focuses on the way, through their power strategies, teachers share and define professional knowledge for each other and how they influence each others' professional activities. It highlights the importance of professional credibility.

Chapter 7, 'Power in the community: teachers and parents', recognises the fact that the work of a teacher involves talking to parents.

This chapter asks: What can we learn about primary teaching by looking at teachers talking to parents? In complete contrast with the previous chapter we see a discussion with parents, in which the teacher chairs and fosters the discussion by adopting less dominant power strategies.

Chapter 8, 'Influences beyond the classroom that affect a teacher's work: power and leadership', considers the external influences upon a teacher's work. It examines a meeting between a headteacher, a local adviser, the deputy head and the language co-ordinator of a primary school who are planning an in-service course. The discussion illustrates many more power strategies. It demonstrates how power strategies limit or facilitate what others can do. Power strategies define the possibilities for the future actions of other people. It illustrates acts of leadership and concludes that, just as a teacher structures the possibilities for the present and future actions of his or her pupils, so the context in which a teacher works is also structured by external power interests.

Chapter 9, 'The influences on teachers' work beyond the school: the wider power context', continues the theme of looking at the power interests which structure the context in which primary teachers perform their professional activities. It takes as a case study the introduction of SATs for seven-year-olds into schools and suggests that teachers are a power group operating amongst other power groups in the wider power context. It attempts to illustrate how the power interests of power groups in the wider power context structure, limit and facilitate what teachers can do, both as a professional group and as individuals in their classrooms.

Chapter 10, 'Teaching and the negotiation of power', returns to the original question: How do primary teachers teach? It concludes that it would be impossible to describe the work of a teacher without taking into account the complex tapestry of power relationships which structure the context of a teacher's professional activities. The power perspective creates an image of a teacher as a power leader in a power situation. It helps us to understand the choices open to teachers and explains how the classroom is managed. It provides us with insights into the professional skills of effective teachers.

At the end of each chapter there are 'Suggestions for teachers'. These activities may be used by teachers on in-service courses, or by teachers who are leading school-based professional development meetings. They may also be useful to individual teachers who are interested in exploring their own professional activities. Finally, they may be of use to those who are involved in teacher education as a means of providing insights, first into the complex power context in which teachers work and, secondly, into the nature of the teacher's professional skills and knowledge.

A note on the research

This was a small-scale research project which initially went into schools to make videos of the kinds of tasks which all teachers perform every day – for example, dismissing the class at lunch time. From these transcriptions the notion of dominant and less dominant identities arose and was applied to situations which were less obviously characteristic of all teachers.

Because there was a difficulty that the videos made for the research purposes might have only recorded the things that the research might want to observe, a second stage was undertaken. In the second stage of the research the analysis of the power relationships was applied to videos which had been taken by other people for other purposes. In this book some of the material has been taken from the first stage of the research and some from the second. An attempt has been made to use a balance of the materials in order to avoid any kind of bias.

Acknowledgements

I am indebted to Professor Michael Newby, Dean of Rolle Faculty of Education, Plymouth University, for his endless patience and constructive comments on successive drafts. I would like to thank colleagues at Rolle Faculty of Education, especially Dr Gordon Taylor and Mrs Gill Payne for their support and encouragement. Thanks also to Dr Andy Hannan and Mr Jeff Lewis for their helpful advice. Finally I would like to thank my family for their patience and understanding through the difficult times.

Thanks to the following for permission to use the following materials: Lampert, Magdalene, How do teachers Manage to Teach? Perspectives on problems in practice *Harvard Educational Review*, Vol 55 no. 2, pp. 178–194 Copyright © 1985 by the President and Fellows of Harvard College; Newspaper Publishing PLC, *The Independent*, *The Guardian*, Times Newspapers Ltd; *The Express and Echo*, Exeter; Dorothy Charlton and Hilary Gallery; BBC Radio for Schools, programme 5, *Building a House*, by Hazel Glynne, 1990; and *Socrates for Six-year-olds*, from the BBC Series *Transformers*, 1990.

1

A dominant identity: power

One of the most interesting questions to ask a teacher is: How do you teach? In the extract which follows a teacher describes her work in the classroom:

> In the school where I teach . . . there are two chalkboards on opposite walls. The students sit at two tables and a few desks, facing in all directions. I rarely sit down while I am teaching except momentarily to offer individual help. Thus the room does not have a stationary 'front' toward which the students can reliably look for directions or lessons from their teacher. Nevertheless an orientation toward one side of the room did develop recently . . . and became the source of some pedagogical problems . . . (Lampert, 1985, p.178).

She talks first about the layout of the classroom and the fact that this gave rise to teaching problems, but then she goes on to talk about the personalities of her pupils:

> The children . . . seem to be allergic to their peers of the opposite sex. Girls rarely choose to be anywhere near a boy, and the boys actively reject the girls whenever possible. This has meant that the boys sit together at the table near one of the blackboards and the girls at the table near the other.
> The fifth grade boys are particularly enthusiastic and boisterous. They engage in discussions of math problems with the same intensity they bring to football. They are talented and work productively under close supervision, but if left to their own devices, their behavior deteriorates and they bully one another, tell loud and silly jokes, and fool around with the math materials . . . (ibid. p.178).

From this point she goes on to describe how she dealt with these problems:

> I developed a habit of routinely curtailing these distractions from the lesson by teaching at the blackboard on the boys' end of the classroom. This enabled me to address the problem of maintaining classroom order

by my physical presence; a cool stare or a touch on the shoulder reminded the boys to give their attention to directions for an activity or to
the content of the lesson, and there was no need to interrupt my teaching.

But my presence near the boys had inadvertently put the girls in 'the
back' of the room. One of the more outspoken girls impatiently pointed
out that she had been trying to get my attention and thought I was
ignoring her. She made me aware that my problem-solving strategy,
devised to keep the boys' attention, had caused another, quite different
problem. The boys could see and hear more easily than the girls and I
noticed their questions more readily. Now what was to be done? (Ibid. p.
178).

A large part of the description of the teacher's concerns about her
classroom was devoted to issues of interpersonal relationships. She
was concerned about the fact that the boys and girls would not sit
together, the fact that the boys were enthusiastic and talented and
their necessary supervision resulted in neglect of the girls. In a different classroom this teacher might have had uppermost in her mind
questions of race, religion, social class, morale, motivation, person-
ality problems or children with special needs.

This teacher also expresses something of her own personal conflict
in the final question: Now what was to be done? Conflicts of this
kind play an important part in the practice of teaching. This point is
well illustrated in the further comments that this teacher makes,
where she reflects upon the situation in her classroom:

When I consider the conflicts that arise in the classroom from my
perspective as a teacher, I do not see a choice between abstract social
goals, such as Excellence versus Equality or Freedom versus Standardiza-
tion. What I see are the tensions between individual students, or personal
confrontations between myself and a particular groups of boys or girls
. . . I cannot see . . . my job as making clear choices. My aims for any one
particular student are tangled with my aims for each of the others in the
class, and more importantly, I am responsible for choosing a course of
action in circumstances where choice leads to further conflict. The contradictions between the goals I am expected to accomplish thus become
continuing inner struggles about how to do my job (*ibid*. pp.181–2).

The comments of this teacher seem to indicate that teaching is an
activity which entails struggling with contradictions.

This teacher makes further comments upon the contradictions
with which she struggles, by describing her role as one of changing
identities. She emphasises the importance of teacher identity in dealing with some of her conflicts:

My ambivalence about what to do was not only a conflict of will,
however, it was a conflict of identity as well. I did not want to be a person

who ignored the girls in my class because the boys were more aggressive in seeking my attention . . . *Working out an identity for this situation was more than a personal concern – it was an essential tool for getting my work done. The kind of person that I am with my students plays an important part in what I am able to accomplish with them.* Figuring out who to be in the classroom is part of my job; by holding the conflicting parts of myself together, I find a way to manage the conflicts in my work. (*ibid.* p.183, emphasis added).

This is an interesting comment because it emphasises the fact that teacher identity can affect what can be accomplished with pupils. It makes us aware of the necessity for teachers to assume different identities in the classroom. One interesting point arising in the first extract indicates that what actually happened in the classroom was not exactly how the teacher would have chosen to operate. However, owing to the combination of the design of the classroom and the personalities of individuals, what actually happened in the classroom was a compromise. It was a compromise in which the teacher attempted to meet the needs of everyone involved, including her own professional need to impart knowledge. Interestingly this teacher never found a solution to her problems, but as the teacher's own reflections indicate, this was not a cause for concern:

A teacher has the potential to act with integrity while maintaining contradictory concerns . . . I managed my dilemma by putting the problems that led to it further into the background and by bringing other parts of my job to the foreground. Although this meant that my problem remained, my strategy gave me a way to live with them (*ibid.* p.185).

From these comments we might conclude that:

- Teaching is an activity of compromise; and
- Teaching is such that attempting to solve one dilemma frequently raises further more serious dilemmas.

In her final comments this teacher attempts to define what she does in the classroom. She describes it as conflict management and concludes that the nature of teaching may present conflicts which require dealing with at three different levels:

[These two stories] portray the teachers as active negotiator, a broker of sorts, balancing a variety of interests that need to be satisfied in classrooms . . . In order to do her job, the dilemma-managing teacher calls upon this conflicted 'self' as a tool of her trade, building a working identity that is constructively ambiguous. While she works at solving society's problems and scholars' problems, she also works at coping with her own internal conflicts. She debates with herself about what to do, and instead of screening out responsibilities that contradict one another, she acknowledges them, embraces the conflict and finds a way to manage. (*ibid*. p.187).

Here we begin to gain an idea of the nature of a teacher's work in the classroom. In order to carry out her professional responsibilities, this teacher suggests that there are three main areas of professional skill required to enable teachers to function effectively:

- Teachers are active negotiators of a range of different interests.
- Teachers succeed by building working identities that are constructively ambiguous.
- Teachers embrace conflict and find ways to manage.

This view of a teacher as a manager, a coper, is an untidy view of teaching. As Lampert points out, for many this is an uncomfortable view since it contradicts deep-seated personal convictions that managing requires the manager to find solutions to problems. Whereas this view of teaching suggests that there may not always be solutions to classroom problems and that the job of the teacher is to devise strategies for preventing more serious problems from surfacing.

Perhaps the most important point that this teacher raises is that she assumes different teaching 'identities', but what does she mean when she says that she assumes an 'identity'?

A dominant identity

One of the easiest kinds of identity to pick out in the classroom is a teacher's dominant identity. We can see this quite clearly in the example of a different teacher who was dismissing her class at morning break.

Teacher: Let's see if everyone else is ready for playtime. (*Rises from the group she has been working with. Sees David.*) You ready for playtime?
David: Yeah . . . I was . . .
Teacher: You look like you're ready for playtime. (*Voice much louder addressing the whole class.*) Right. Stand behind your chairs. (*Children begin to stand up. Some put their hands together for prayers.*) David! (*emphatically.*) . . . Stand still! (*Looks at the group tidying up.*) No. Do that during playtime . . . You ready Richard? (*Looks around and sees the children with their hands together.*) No, not lunch time. Michael's putting his hands together. He's hoping it's lunch time . . . Just waiting for David to stand still. (*Looks about the room.*) Very still, David. (*Long silence. Then in a very soft voice.*) Right. Off you go quietly. (*Children exit in an orderly manner.*)

If we look carefully at what this teacher actually says we shall be able to pick out the strategies she uses. Two of the strategies which are clear from the video, but which are difficult to illustrate in writing, are that she uses a louder voice and a dominant rising tone (Brazil, 1978). She uses many 'Rights', which tell the children that something new is about to begin (Sinclair and Coulthard, 1975). She also uses ritual language and routines with which the children are familiar. She says: 'Stand behind your chairs . . .', a routine which the children perform regularly before they go out to play. We also get a glimpse of the further lunch-time routine of saying prayers, when the children automatically, but mistakenly, put their hands together ready to say prayers. The teacher insists that the children stand still and are quiet before she lowers her voice, uses another 'Right', and the familiar dismissal phrase: 'Off you go quietly.'

Throughout the whole of this routine children are not invited to comment, only to do as they are told. To bring this about the teacher uses dominant power strategies:

- The teacher uses ritual language and routine actions to control the situation.
- The teacher uses a dominant rising tone to hold the floor and inhibit interruption from the children.
- The teacher uses contrasts in the loudness and softness of her voice as a further control measure.
- She does not encourage participation from the children, but expects them to stand quietly and listen for her to dismiss them.

Later in the morning the same teacher prepares for lunch time:

Teacher: Right, it's dinnertime. Right. Listen. This is what I want you to do, carefully. Those people with sheets and books, in a minute, when I tell you, you can just put those things away and check the floor for rubbers, sharpeners, pens, etc. Right. (*Children rise. Very high voice and rising tone . . .*) I haven't said move. Just because they're moving. (*Indicates the class next door.*) Mark and Richard I am not happy that you have done enough work this morning. So you can spend some of your lunch time making up for some of the work you haven't done. When I think you've done enough, I shall let you go . . . But you need to make up the time. (*Mark mutters inaudibly. She puts her hand upon his head as if to restrain him.*) And all of the time you yap, you're wasting time. (*He jerks his head from underneath her hand resentfully. She looks away and addresses the rest of the class.*) The rest of you can pack away. Could I have some volunteers to pack this away, please? (*Indicates the maths apparatus.*)
Children: I will . . . I will . . . (*The teacher looks at two children across the room.*)
Teacher: Well pack your things up first and then come and do it.

Here we see similar dominant power strategies for controlling the situation. This time there are many more 'Rights', and a 'Listen'. We can also pick out ritual phrases, such as: 'this is what I want you to do, in a minute, when I tell you, I haven't said move,' which were all spoken in a dominant rising tone. Again the teacher has adopted a very dominant identity and a dominant position with the children. We can see that the teacher is employing verbal strategies to prevent the children from interrupting her.

Here we can begin to see what it is about these strategies which makes the 'dominant' rather than anything else:

- A dominant strategy is 'dominant' because it has particular effects upon the children.
- Dominant strategies are all strategies which limit or close down the possibilities for the future action of the children.
- They limit what the children can or cannot do.

If we look at the next section of the transcription, we can see how the dominant strategies limit what can happen next. It is interesting that at this point the teacher chooses to perform what is probably her most dominant act directed at individuals during the course of the whole morning. She announces that Mark and Richard will be expected to stay in at lunch time and make up for the time they have lost. Again she uses familiar strategies. She presents a situation, problem, solution and evaluation (Hoey, 1979):

> SITUATION AND PROBLEM
> Mark and Richard I am not happy that you have done enough work this morning.
> SOLUTION
> So you can spend some of your lunch time making up for some of the work you haven't done. When I think you've done enough, I shall let you go . . .
> EVALUATION
> But you need to make up the time.

The loud rising tones in which the teacher makes this pronouncement make it quite clear that this is what is going to happen. There can be no doubt, or debating the matter. In other words, Mark and Richard have their possibilities for future action limited to this course, and this course only. This is a very dominant strategy, owing to the effects it has upon Mark and Richard.

However, this is not the end of the matter. Mark mutters a protest and this is very interesting because it illustrates the fact that dominant strategies in the classroom are not the sole prerogative of the teacher. Mark has behaved in a very dominant way, his protest has set up the possibility of a confrontation, which the teacher must now deal with. This example illustrates the point that children may also operate dominant strategies upon their teacher, and that the power relationship in the process of teaching and learning is a two-way process.

At this point there is a possibility of a confrontation breaking out, so how does the teacher deal with it? '(*Mark mutters inaudibly. She puts her hand upon his head as if to restrain him.*) And all of the time you yap, you're wasting time.'

She restrains him physically, then repeats an evaluation, as if to insist that this is the end of the matter. Mark, although at this point he will not verbally contest the power relationships he does so non-verbally: '*He jerks his head from underneath her hand resentfully.*'

At this point the teacher adopts a disengaging strategy by ignoring Mark. She looks away and addresses the rest of the class, then completely changes the subject, so that there can be no further discussion in: 'The rest of you can pack away. Could I have some volunteers to pack this away, please?'

This is a very powerful move. Mark no longer has the attention of the teacher: in her disengagement she has abandoned his interests. In effect she has been obliged to adopt a further dominant strategy to contain Mark's protest.

From these examples we begin to see that when a teacher assumes a dominant identity she uses dominant power strategies. Dominant strategies limit the possibilities of further action for the other participants. The dominant strategies used by the teacher and pupils in this extract were as follows:

- Using ritual language.
- Using predictable routines to control groups of children.
- Using contrasts in the loudness and softness of her voice.
- Using dominant rising tones.
- Using body language to control attempts at contesting the power outcome.
- Changing the subject.
- Using strategies of disengagement.
- Protesting.
- Continually establishing and re-establishing a state of consent and co-operation between the teacher and pupils.
- Curtailing contributions from some pupils to allow others to speak.

(See the dominant teacher identity chart, Figure 1.1.)

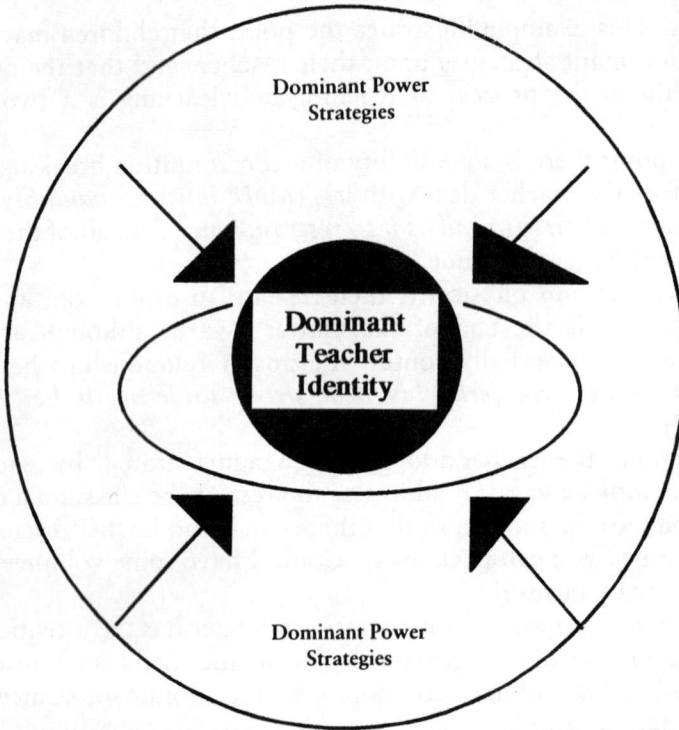

Figure 1.1 A dominant teacher identity is defined by dominant power strategies

Suggestions for teachers

1. Think about a class that you have taught recently. What were your main professional concerns?
2. How would you describe your teacher identity with this class?
3. Did your teacher identity change at all during the lesson? In what ways did it change? What caused it to change?
4. What kind of demands do you make upon your pupils? In what ways do you co-operate with your pupils in order to allow learning to proceed?
5. What kind of demands do your pupils make upon you? In what ways do your pupils co-operate with you in order to allow learning to proceed?
6. In what ways do you think your teacher identity might be the same as your personal identity? In what ways does your identity differ when you are in the classroom?

2

A less dominant identity: power by consent

In the last chapter we saw how the teacher adopted dominant power strategies which limited what could be done and the kinds of contribution that could be made. However, this is not the only kind of situation that teachers have to deal with. Sometimes, for example, teachers talk about handing over the learning to their pupils. In the extract which follows a different teacher set out to hold a discussion in which the children could develop their own knowledge in their own ways. What can this tell us about the power strategies of a teacher? (The transcription is from a BBC documentary, *Socrates for Six Year Olds*, transcribed in the second stage of the research. The names have been changed for confidentiality.) This group of six-year-old children were sitting quite formally on their chairs in a circle. Before the discussion started the teacher reminded the children about the rules that everyone had agreed to observe:

1. Everyone would sit still and stay in their place.
2. Only one person could speak at once.
3. Anyone who wanted to speak must put up their hand.

The children chose the topic of the discussion. They began talking about the brain and how it might work:

Alex: . . . your brain is for learn . . . and powerful . . .
Teacher: So you agree with Geoffrey who says your brain thinks and you don't agree with Catherine who says it's you that thinks . . . not your brain? That's an interesting thing to say, Catherine . . . (*Long eye contact.*)
David: It's a connection . . .
Teacher: It's a connection, you're right David . . . (*Smiles.*) . . . Charles . . .
Charles: Well I disagree with Catherine because if you didn't have a brain . . . you wouldn't be thinking about the words that I'm talking right now, so it would be impossible without your brain.
Catherine: I think it could be possible for your brain, because you have a heart and your heart can beat, and it can think that it's beating.

Teacher: Barry . . . (*Smiles, long eye contact.*)
Barry: If you . . . if your heart beats, that's just your heart beating. You don't know if your heart thinks . . .
Teacher: You don't know if your heart thinks . . .
Barry: And if . . . if you . . . if you have . . . your brain, like we really do . . . you would know all the thoughts.
Teacher: (*Smiles, falling then rising tone, long drawn out.*) O-o-kay. (*Gently.*) . . . Linda . . .
Linda: I agree with Charles because you think like . . . and your brain stores your thoughts.

Perhaps the most striking observation to be made from this extract is that these six-year-old children are having such an interesting conversation. The teacher plays very little part in what is happening, and therefore appears to have no control over the situation. It raises the question of what influence the teacher's identity and power strategies have on this situation. In complete contrast to the lesson (pp.4–5), the teacher does not dominate the conversation or attempt to hold the floor. Throughout the whole discussion she makes only seven contributions which are quite short.

In her first contribution she simply restates what Alex has said. Her voice was very gentle and she established long eye contact with Alex. In her second contribution the teacher turned to David and said encouragingly: 'It's a connection, you're right David . . . (*Smiles.*) . . . Charles . . .'

Here we see the same identity offering encouragement, as similarly in her next contribution: 'Barry . . . (*Smiles, long eye contact.*)' In her fourth comment the teacher seems to support Barry, who begins a contribution and seems unable to finish it. The teacher repeats his contribution, as if to remind him of his last point and pauses: 'You don't know if your heart thinks . . .' Barry is then able to continue and finish what he was going to say.

From this point the discussion continues:

Teacher: So it's really you that's doing the thinking. (*Linda nods. Teacher smiles. Long eye contact.*) Oh, okay. Robert . . .
Robert: Well . . . if you didn't have a brain you wouldn't be able to say, what's that poem? (*Points to a poem on the wall.*) What's that . . .? (*Points to the floor. General outbreak of comments and hubbub.*)
John: (*Excited.*) How would you know it what was happening, and how would you know how to spell the word if you didn't think about the word . . .
Peter: (*Interrupts.*) I don't know anything, so you won't . . . you won't know what you're saying . . . and you like, you don't know it.
Teacher: So you can't even say: 'What's that . . ? 'Is that what you say, Peter?
Peter: Yeah . . .

Clive: Yeah, because if you don't know it, it's like . . . well I don't know what that is, and you don't know if . . . you don't even know where you are . . .
Peter: (*Interrupts excitedly.*) You won't even know how to say 'what's that?' . . . you can't even talk.
Clive: I know . . . (*Laughs.*) . . . you can't even talk because you don't know what the words are . . .
Teacher: David . . .

The teacher's fifth contribution is interesting. Throughout the discussion we have seen her encouraging the children to take a dominant position in the discussion. In the extract, dominant acts were brought about by producing a whole discourse sequence of situation, problem, solution and evaluation. In order to produce dominant acts with dominant power relationships it is important that the children learn to produce an utterance with a complete discourse structure. The children clearly do not find this easy. When they forget where they are up to the teacher reminds them. If they lose track of their contribution and miss parts of the structure out, she gently puts it in for them. We see this happening in the following:

Barry: If you . . . if your heart beats, that's just your heart beating. You don't know if your heart thinks . . .
Teacher: You don't know if your heart thinks . . .
Barry: And if . . . if you . . . if you have . . . your brain, like we really do . . . you would know all the thoughts.
Teacher: (*Smiles, falling then rising tone, long drawn out.*) O-o-kay. (*Gently.*) . . . Linda . . .

In his first contribution Barry manages a situation and a problem, but then falters. The teacher reminds him of the state of play by repeating his point. She does not attempt to influence his thinking in any way. Barry then continues with a solution but does not include an evaluation. The teacher carefully puts this in for him with 'O-o-kay'. This was not the ordinary evaluation which teachers give when evaluating children's performances. She used a special fall-rising tone in her voice suggesting: 'That's it, that's all you are going to say, is it?' The teacher then proceeded to name the next child who would contribute. Selecting the next child to contribute is an important strategy. We see it happening after Linda's contribution:

Linda: I agree with Charles because you think like . . . and your brain stores your thoughts.
Teacher: So it's really you that's doing the thinking. (*Linda nods. Teacher smiles. Long eye contact.*) Oh, okay. Robert . . .

Linda was unable to produce a complete sequence. In order to help her, the teacher reiterated Linda's position. She re-established Linda amongst the other participants so that the contribution could be properly finished, but Linda only nodded her assent. When this happened the teacher carefully put in the evaluation in: 'Oh, okay', then she proceeded to select the child who was going to make the next contribution. We see the same happening in the teacher's exchange with Peter:

> *Peter:* (*Interrupts.*) I don't know anything, so you won't . . . you won't know what you're saying . . . and you like, you don't know it.
> *Teacher:* So you can't even say: 'What's that . . ?' Is that what you say, Peter?
> *Peter:* Yeah . . .

Here the teacher asks a direct question, thus obliging Peter to make the required evaluation. As the discussion continues, the children begin to take responsibility for what is happening themselves:

> *David:* Erm . . . well . . . I can, I can, I think I can sort of answer . . . answer . . . erm . . . the question, because if you didn't have a brain . . . you would keep falling down . . . y-y-you would keep falling down into the street, and you would get run over . . . so you would just be immediately dead, if you can't have a brain . . .
> *Catherine:* I disagree . . . erm . . . with David, because you would . . . walk . . . and . . . I disagree with Paul . . .
> *David:* (*Interrupts.*) . . . yeah, but . . . your brain would tell you, to walk, I'm thinking that I've gotta talk . . . and if I didn't have a brain I wouldn't be talking . . . or I . . . or if (*excited*) I didn't have a brain I couldn't hear you and I wouldn't be here . . . and I wouldn't be at school. (*Pauses and smiles at the thought.*) I wouldn't be doing anything . . . I wouldn't be alive . . .

Although the children had difficulty putting together their thoughts and expressing them, we can see that this did not stop them from having a serious discussion. In the last exchange the exchange structure of the discourse is shared between several participants:

SITUATION
Clive: Yeah, because if you don't know it, it's like . . .
PROBLEM
. . . well I don't know what that is and you don't know if . . . you don't even know where you are . . .
Peter: (*Interrupts excitedly.*) You won't even know how to say 'what's that?' . . . you can't even talk.
Clive: I know . . . (*Laughs.*) . . . you can't even talk because you don't know what the words are . . .
Teacher: David . . .
SOLUTION
David: Erm . . . well . . . I can, I can, I think I can sort of answer . . . answer . . . erm . . . the question, because if you didn't have a brain . . .

you would keep falling down . . . y-y-you would keep falling down into the street, and you would get run over . . .
EVALUATION
so you would just be immediately dead, if you can't have a brain . . .

Here we see the children truly sharing the responsibility for the discourse. No single child makes a dominant act of producing an utterance with a complete discourse sequence. To the contrary, each contribution is relevant to what has gone before and develops the discourse with an appropriate structural element. It demonstrates that even very young children are perfectly able to hold a discussion if appropriate opportunities are created for them to do so. But what are these opportunities and how are they created? How can we describe what this teacher is doing?

First, the teacher did not initiate the topic of conversation and during the discussion she does not attempt to dominate or hold the floor. In relation to the children she makes very short contributions. All of her contributions, far from trying to limit or control what the children can do, are concerned with restating the children's position, and helping them to develop their contribution in any way that they can. In effect she creates new opportunities for the children to develop and extend their contributions. We might say that in her interventions this teacher creates new opportunities for action.

Far from limiting the possibilities for future action, this teacher is facilitating new opportunities. She is creating new chances for the children to improve upon, or put right their performance. We might therefore say that this teacher has adopted a less dominant identity and less dominant power strategies.

In different circumstances, for example, if the discussion had deteriorated to a point where the teacher considered that it was no longer educationally valuable, then we might have seen different strategies from the teacher. But in this particular example, at no point does the teacher attempt to steer the conversation or influence the thinking. Her main concern seems to be to keep the discussion going, to create further opportunities for the children to develop their learning. (See the less dominant teacher identity chart, Figure 2.1.)

At this point we can draw some contrasts between this teacher and the teacher dismissing her class at lunch time (p.5). Interestingly, both of them used the strategy of evaluation, but they used it in different ways and for different purposes. In Chapter 2 the teacher used evaluations as a signal that this is the end of the matter whereas, in this discussion, the evaluation is never the end of the matter. This teacher provides evaluations, but they are evaluations of the discussion itself, and not of how well the children have performed. She

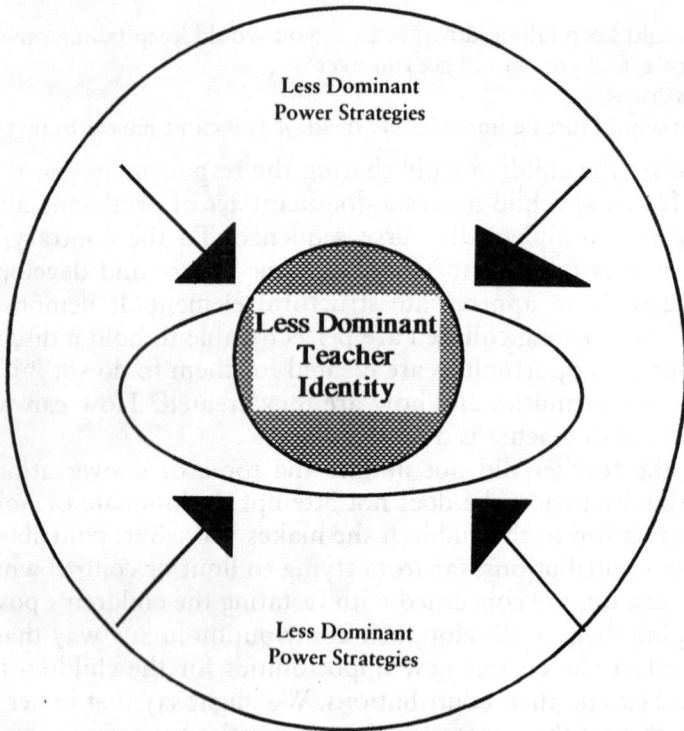

Figure 2.1 A less dominant teacher identity is defined by less dominant power strategies

provides evaluations only to enable the discourse to proceed and, interestingly, the evaluations are always followed by another move. We can see this in '(*Smiles, falling then rising tone, long drawn out.*) O-o-kay. (*Gently.*) . . . Linda . . .' and 'So it's really you that's doing the thinking. (*Linda nods. Teacher smiles. Long eye contact.*) Oh, okay. Robert . . .

Each time the teacher makes an evaluation she immediately selects a child to begin the next exchange. That is, she never leaves the discourse at a point where it might be considered complete, always at a point where it is incomplete. In this way she encourages and facilitates the continuation of the discussion. She is manipulating the structure of the discourse in a different way from the teacher in the previous extracts (p.5).

In the previous extract (p.5) we saw how the teacher controlled the situation by dominating it or holding the floor, but this does not appear to be happening in this discussion. In this discussion the children hold the floor and are dominant. The teacher's strategies are all aimed at facilitating the discussion. We see her adopting less dominant power strategies and relying heavily on the co-operation of the children. So how might we describe this teacher's less dominant power strategies?

The teacher's power strategies

This teacher adopted a less dominant identity, and we saw her using correspondingly less dominant power strategies. Her strategies involved the following:

- Selecting the next contributor to the discussion.
- Ensuring that the discussion continued.
- Restating the children's position when they 'lost track' of what was happening.
- Being extremely well organised.
- Having very high expectations of the children.
- Making her expectations clear to the children.
- Setting out precise rules about how the children should behave during the activity.
- Trusting the children and respecting their contributions to the discussion.
- Encouraging children's efforts.
- Anticipating difficulties and providing positive support when help was needed.
- Keeping quiet and allowing the children to take responsibility for the discussion.
- Exercising restraint on her own impulses to lead and direct the discussion.

Interestingly, the variety of less dominant strategies used by teachers is far greater than the range of dominant strategies.

The list of skills which this particular teacher was using highlights the fact that in adopting less dominant power relationships the teacher had to produce a far more structured situation in the classroom. She needed to know exactly what she was setting out to achieve and exactly how she was going to achieve it. From these points, we begin to realise very quickly that adopting less dominant power strategies in the classroom is far from taking the easy way out. It would have been far easier for this teacher to walk into her classroom and direct the learning activities. Instead she chose to exercise far more personal control and expected her class to exercise similar restraint in their dealings with each other. From the example of this teacher we might infer that

- adopting less dominant power strategies requires the teacher to have a clear view of what he or she wants the children to achieve and how he or she will help them to achieve it; and
- adopting less dominant power strategies means that the teacher must provide a structured learning environment which will make it possible for the children to be challenged, but also to be successful.

Suggestions for teachers

1. Try making a video recording or audio recording of a lesson that you have taught:
   (a) Working with individual children.
   (b) Working with a small group.
   (c) Teaching the whole class.
   If this is not possible try recalling the last lesson you taught.
2. Look at the list of less dominant power strategies that this teacher used. Do you use these strategies? Can you find examples of them in your specimen lesson?
3. Can you find examples of different strategies that you may have used?
4. Make a list of the strategies that you routinely perform.
5. Are there any strategies which you use more frequently than others?
6. Does the teacher in the extract use any power strategies that you do not use?
7. Do you use particular power strategies with particular children or groups of children? How do you decide on the best ways of handling a situation?
8. If you are working with other teachers, try asking them to observe your power strategies and allowing you to observe theirs. In what ways are they the same? In what ways are they different? Can you explain why there may be differences or similarities?

3

Constructively ambiguous identities: the operation of power in the classroom

We have seen illustrations of a dominant teacher identity expressed in dominant power strategies, and a less dominant teacher identity expressed in less dominant power strategies. However, anyone who has ever taught in a classroom would quickly protest that primary teachers spend a very small part of their day dismissing children at break times, and holding class discussions. What happens for example, when teachers have simultaneous group and individual activities running in their classrooms? How do power strategies operate in these situations?

The extract which follows is a transcription of a video of a primary school teacher working in her classroom. What can it tell us about the teacher's identity? (All of the names have been changed in the transcription to preserve anonymity.) The teacher in this small rural primary school had organised a variety of activities for her class of 26 seven-year-olds. The tables were arranged in four islands in the middle of the room, but some children were also working individually on worktops around the walls. Some children were working on their own, whilst others were working in small groups. The teacher was circulating the groups offering advice and assistance. At the point where the transcription begins the teacher approached a group of four children who were playing a maths game using Diennes apparatus. The rules of the game were that only a certain number of 'flats' could be taken before the player went 'bust', but the children were having difficulty understanding this.

> *Teacher:* No. Nobody has to miss a go. You just – yeah – no, it's just it means you miss the turn you're on. So if you go bust you can't do anything, can you? So you actually leave that go. (*Pauses and looks around the group. Sees that Emily appears to have a complete set of 'flats'.*) Have you made it? Oh, well done! She's done it. You didn't go bust did you?
> *Alison:* Yes she did . . .

Barbara: She did . . . (*together.*)

Teacher: No, I mean did you go bust to make that? (*Emily does not reply, looks confused.*)

Alison: Yeah . . .

Teacher: Shh-hh. Let her tell me. Let her tell me . . .

Emily: I didn't . . . I . . .

Teacher: (*Leaning over the table to Emily.*) What was your last throw? (*Long silence.*) What did you throw just now? (*Emily does not reply*).

Alison: She didn't throw anything . . .

Barbara: We thought you said just go . . .

Teacher: No, no, no. What did you throw just now? How have you made that?

Colin: I thought you meant . . . she has . . . she had . . . she had a bit of er . . . She had two flats . . . and she put on something . . . but she took off more than she put on.

Teacher: Mmm. (*Nods to Colin, then turns to Emily.*) How many did you get just now? How many flats? How many units did you get just now? Can you remember? (*Emily shakes her head.*)

Colin: Yes, she got five . . .

Alison: She's bust because she's got four.

Teacher: I think what has happened is you've gone over, Emily. All right? You've had too many. Right? Let's just take one off, look. Let's take one off. Right? Now what you need Emily is . . . You need one flat, or less than that. If you have more than that, you can't go. All right? You mustn't have more than that. You can only have up as far as one whole block. The minute you go over . . . you can't go. You have got to get the exact amount. Okay?

(*Susie approaches. She has been working on her own, doing addition sums which she has finished.*)

(*Very soft voice.*) What is it, Susie? (*Susie looks bashful and mutters inaudibly.*)

Come on then Susie. You have finished. Well done. Let's see. (*Susie returns to her seat and the teacher leans right over her head to mark the work.*) Coo-oo . . . You did those quickly, didn't you? (*Continues marking.*) Tell me, how many is eight and five?

Susie: (*Long silence. Then shyly . . .*) Twelve . . . (*Teacher bends down to Susie's eye level. Their heads very close together.*)

Teacher: Tell me how you are working it out.

Susie: Well, I'm thinking of five . . . and adding on . . .

Teacher: You're thinking of five and adding on eight. Let me hear you do it then . . .

Susie: . . . Five, six, seven, eight, nine, ten, eleven . . .

Teacher: How many. . . How do you know how many you have added on?

Susie: Cos . . . erm . . . Well you see . . .

Teacher: I can't add on in my head . . .

Peter: Ow! (*Teacher and Susie turn and look in the direction of the disturbance.*)

Teacher: (*Loud sharp voice.*) Is there a problem?

Barry: (*Indignant.*) He kicked the leg of my chair . ..

Teacher: Yeah, I don't blame him because you're pushing right in front of him. Would you like to sit back a bit? Right. (*Emphatically wagging a finger.*)

Now I'm not going to talk to either of you, until I have finished with Susie. So you might as well go away (*motions away with her hand. Peter goes.*) . . . and put your hand up when you can see I have finished with Susie. (*Turns to Barry very emphatically.*) And you can do the same because I am not talking to you until I have finished with Susie. Okay? (*Barry protests inaudibly.*) Well you'll just have to wait. (*Very firmly, voice louder and rising.*) You'll just have to wait, won't you? (*Turns back to Susie. Very soft voice.*) . . . I can't add on in my head. I would need to use something to add on, like my ruler or my fingers. That's what you normally do, don't you? Are you using your fingers under the table?

Susie: (*Smiles and looks at the teacher.*) Yeah.

Teacher: (*Very gently*) I thought you were . . . (*Susie grins broadly.*) I could see your li'le fingers moving. (*Teacher and Susie grin at each other.*) Now you show me how you're gonna add on . . . Why don't you start with eight and add on five. Start with the big number then you haven't got so many to add on.

Susie: (*Long think.*) . . . thirteen . . .

Teacher: Thirteen . . . That's very good. Well done. Did you use your fingers under the table? (*Susie grins and nods. Teacher grins.*) I thought you did! (*Susie and the teacher grin at each other. Long eye contact. Teacher stands up.*) That's okay. (*Pats Susie on the shoulder.*)

Susie: What should I do now? (*Teacher bends over towards Susie.*)

Teacher: Maths. All right? Okay. You can go on with your other. (*Another child approaches and waits patiently.*) . . . Try and remember when you're adding on . . . if you start with the big number . . . you haven't got so many to add on, have you? So instead of starting with five and adding on eight . . . start with eight and add on five, okay? Good girl. (*Teacher turns and walks away towards another group. The child who has been waiting follows her.*) Right? (*Addressing the new group.*)

Andrew: Please miss . . . we don't understand . . .

Teacher: Having a problem? (*The child who has been following her now moves in front of her and touches her arm. She puts her hand on his shoulder.*) All right. I'll just see to David because he was next and then I will come to you. (*Walks over to David's table. David sits down and she proceeds to look at his work.*) Oh you see . . . Look at the difference, David! Isn't that good! You can really see how much you've improved, can't you? You've worked ever so hard. Good boy. I should think you're proud of that aren't you? (*Enthusiastically.*) Yeah! Good boy. (*Moves away from David's table and is immediately addressed by Louise.*)

Louise: Miss Steven's . . . erm . . . (*Looks awkward.*) Can I work on a different table where I can get more work done please? (*Long silence as teacher thinks.*)

Teacher: (*Hesitantly suspicious.*) Yeah. Is there a problem?

Louise: Yeah . . . well . . . erm . . . Jane keeps on nudging me with her arm, by accident . . . (*demonstrates*) like that . . .

Teacher: (*Understanding.*) Oh. You're a bit squashed, are you? Okay. Yes. You can go and work in the quiet corner if you like. (*Turns to Jane and smiles.*) There you are, Jane, you can have all your elbow room now. (*Walks away to maths group with earlier problem.*) Right. What's the problem?

From this extract we see a primary school teacher moving from one interaction to another between groups and between individuals. First she talks to the maths group and explains the game then she moves on to talk to Susie, but this interaction is disrupted by an argument between Peter and Barry. When the conversation with Susie is finished the teacher moves on to a further group, but delays dealing with their problems until she has looked at David's work. Then Louise asks if she can move to another part of the room. Finally the teacher goes back to a group who were having difficulties with their work. On close examination, we can see how the teacher adopts constructively ambiguous teacher identities.

Power strategies with individuals

From this extract it was clear that the teacher controlled the possibilities for individual pupils in differing degrees. She sets up different kinds of power relationships with different children. With Susie for example, she was less dominant, and she set up a less dominant power relationship, which allowed room for exploring ideas. There was space for the sharing of humour, advice, praise, explanation and evaluation.

When Susie approaches, she has had difficulty with her maths, and the teacher responds speaking in a very soft voice, leans right over the child completely enclosing her, makes encouraging comments: 'Coo-oo . . . You did those quickly, didn't you?' Most of this interaction is carried out with the teacher bending right down with her face very close to Susie's face. When Susie takes a long time to answer the teacher's questions, the teacher waits.

The teacher finds that Susie had difficulty adding five on to eight. She does not just explain the difficulty, but works it out with Susie in: 'Tell me how you are working it out.' Later in the interaction she teases a little: 'Are you using your fingers under the table?'

There is a marked change in the language of the teacher at this point. She begins to use more casual forms of address:

Are you using your fingers under the table?
Susie: (Smiles and looks at the teacher.) Yeah.
Teacher: (Very gently). I thought you were . . . (Susie grins broadly.) I could see your li'le fingers moving. (Teacher and Susie grin at each other.) Now you show me how you're gonna add on . . .

The teacher refers to Susie's 'li'le fingers' and then she says 'tell me how you're gonna add on'. This reinforces the friendly supportive attitude adopted by the teacher in her non-verbal communication.

The fingers become a point of contact between the child and the teacher who share several grins about it and have extended eye contact.

During the interaction the teacher makes helpful and supportive comments: 'I can't add on in my head. I would need to use something to add on, like my ruler or my fingers. That's what you normally do, don't you?'

When Susie answers the question correctly the teacher is full of praise and encouragement: 'Thirteen . . . That's very good. Well done. Did you use your fingers under the table? (*Susie grins and nods. Teacher grins.*) I thought you did! (*Susie and the teacher grin at each other. Long eye contact. Teacher stands up.*) That's okay. (*Pats Susie on the shoulder.*)' And: '. . . Try and remember when you're adding on . . . if you start with the big number . . . you haven't got so many to add on, have you? So instead of starting with five and adding on eight . . . start with eight and add on five, okay? Good girl.'

With David and Emily the teacher was doing the talking and the children were expected to listen. The teacher was far more dominant and the children had far less room to respond in any way other than the way the teacher expected them to respond. For example, she said to David: 'Oh you see . . . Look at the difference, David! Isn't that good! You can really see how much you've improved, can't you? You've worked ever so hard. Good boy. I should think you're proud of that, aren't you? (*Enthusiastically.*) Yeah! Good boy.'

Given this *fait accompli* there was very little David could have added. It would have been very difficult for him to do anything other than accept what the teacher said and she made it clear in her final evaluation 'Good boy' that there really was no more to be said. Here there are dominant power strategies.

The most dominant power strategies appeared in the interaction with Barry and Peter. First there was a disruption which caught the attention of the teacher. In a loud rising dominant tone she asked: 'Is there a problem?' Already she had assumed a dominant identity when Barry protested indignantly that his chair had been kicked. Here there was a potential confrontation developing and what did the teacher do about it? She adopted a less dominant identity to 'defuse' the situation. She signals her less dominant identity with greater informality in the language: 'Yeah, I don't blame him . . .' Then she adopts a very polite, even less dominant identity. 'Would you like to sit back a bit?' These two moves effectively defuse the argument. As soon as this is done the teacher signals a new start in the discourse with another 'Right'. Having brought the situation under control she can now do something about structuring the possibilities for the future actions of the two aggressive boys. She does this in no uncertain terms by combining body language, tone, pitch and loudness of voice and very emphatic use of language:

> Right. (*Emphatically wagging a finger.*) Now I'm not going to talk to either of you, until I have finished with Susie. So you might as well go away (*motions away with her hand. Peter goes*) . . . and put your hand up when you can see I have finished with Susie. (*Turns to Barry very emphatically.*) And you can do the same because I am not talking to you until I have finished with Susie. Okay?

Here she presented a whole discourse sequence of situation, problem, solution and evaluation (Hoey, 1979). Effectively this should have been the end of the matter. With her final evaluation the teacher was signalling that this was definitely the end of the matter and there was nothing more to be said. This was a very dominant strategy because it was so final. She expected Barry to do exactly as he had been told, but Barry protested. Immediately the teacher stepped in with a dominant rising tone, a loud firm voice, and emphatic language, which she repeated to be certain that he had understood her point: 'Well you'll just have to wait. (*Very firmly, voice louder and rising.*) You'll just have to wait, won't you?' This repetition was a particularly dominant strategy on the part of the teacher which left no room at all for Barry to respond and this time this really was the end of the matter.

From these examples we can begin to see how, as a general rule, teachers avoid confrontation in the classroom. But if a confrontation should arise there are several dominant power strategies that teachers may adopt:

- Teachers may use repetition to control the behaviour of their pupils.
- Teachers may use a dominant rising tone of voice.
- Teachers may use emphatic language.
- Teachers use the structure of the discourse to circumscribe the possibilities of future actions for their pupils.

This is a particularly interesting interaction because we can see how the teacher quickly assesses the power relationships at the beginning to see if there is a problem. Next we see her operate within the existing power relationships as she adopts a less dominant strategy to defuse the situation. Then finally she renegotiates the power relationships in such a way that the only future outcome can be one of bringing the confrontation to an end. At this point we can begin to glimpse the skill of a teacher who so adeptly manipulates the power outcome of the situation: teachers assess the state of play in the power situation and the most effective identity to operate within the power constraints. Then they restructure the power outcome of the situation.

From these examples we begin to gain an impression of how the teacher manipulates the power relationships with her pupils in order to get her work done. Her handling of each individual is inconsistent in relation to the other individuals in the class, but consistent with each child. She allots each individual a place in the power situation, which will enable her to proceed with her professional activity of encouraging learning.

However, the teacher does not always work with individuals.

Power strategies with small groups

In her work with the maths group she structured the possibilities for the other participants in different ways. When the teacher operates with groups or individuals we see her first asking questions which enable her to gather information quickly, and assess the state of play in the power situation. With the maths group she said: 'You didn't go bust did you? . . . No, I mean did you go bust to make that?'

At the beginning of her conversation with Susie she says: 'What is it, Susie? . . . You have finished. Well done. Let's see . . . Tell me, how many is eight and five? . . . how you are working it out.'

In the interaction with Peter and Barry she asks: 'Is there a problem?' With the group who are experiencing difficulties she quickly assesses the state of play with: 'Right? Having a problem?'

Here we can see how the teacher's questioning technique is not only important to her pupils' learning but also crucial to her control of what happens in the classroom. If she does not ask the right questions, she will not get the information she needs about the state of play in the power situation: teachers assess the state of play in the power situation by careful questioning.

Once she has assessed the state of play the teacher then proceeds to manage the power relationships. For example in the discussion with the maths group we see her inhibiting contributions from Alison and Barbara, whilst encouraging Emily to take part:

Teacher: Shh-hh. Let her tell me. Let her tell me . . .
Emily: I didn't . . . I . . .
Teacher: (*Leaning over the table to Emily.*) What was your last throw? (*Long silence.*) What did you throw just now? (*Emily does not reply.*)

Teachers inhibit the contributions of some pupils in order to encourage the participation of others.

In this action the teacher has created a new learning opportunity for Emily, but Emily was unable to respond to it.

When there was no obvious solution to the problem of how Emily had acquired so many 'flats', the teacher used another strategy to structure the situation in such a way that the learning could quickly continue. She adopts a strategy of demonstrating superior knowledge to settle the argument over whether or not Emily had gone bust:

> I think what has happened is you've gone over, Emily. All right? You've had too many. Right? Let's just take one off, look. Let's take one off. Right? Now what you need Emily is . . . You need one flat, or less than that. If you have more than that, you can't go. All right? You mustn't have more than that. You can only have up as far as one whole block. The minute you go over . . . you can't go. You have got to get the exact amount. Okay?

Here she has clearly manipulated the structure of the discourse to try to inhibit further discussion and enable the activity to continue, but she does not do this by force. She presents a situation, problem, solution and in the final 'Right?' 'All right?' 'Okay?' she creates opportunities for the children to comment, but she only encourages comments of a particular kind. The position of the children in this power situation is to make evaluative comments. In this way the teacher has tightly controlled the discussion and the kinds of comments she is prepared to accept from the children. The fact that the children do not comment is taken by the teacher as a sign of consent to continue:

- Teachers can control the kinds of comments that they are prepared to accept from children by manipulating the structure of the discourse.
- Teachers may use the structure of the power situation to establish and re-establish continually a state of consent between the teacher and pupils.

Similarly in the conversation with Louise the language helps us to see the strategies used by the teacher for structuring the power outcome of the situation:

> *Louise:* Miss Steven's . . . erm . . .(*Looks awkward.*) Can I work on a different table where I can get more work done please? (*Long silence as teacher thinks.*)
> *Teacher:* (*Hesitantly suspicious.*) Yeah. Is there a problem?
> *Louise:* Yeah . . . well . . . erm . . . Jane keeps on nudging me with her arm, by accident . . . (*demonstrates*) like that . . .
> *Teacher:* (*Understanding.*) Oh. You're a bit squashed, are you? Okay. Yes. You can go and work in the quiet corner if you like. (*Turns to Jane and smiles.*) There you are, Jane, you can have all your elbow room now.

Louise presents the teacher with a situation but the teacher is suspicious. She asks: 'Is there a problem?' Louise proceeds to explain the problem. The teacher then provides a solution and evaluation, indicating again that this is the end of the matter and there will be no further reprisals for 'nudging elbows'. Here the teacher has quickly assessed the situation, worked within its constraints and restructured the power situation in such a way that both of the girls are aware that there is no further problem. It is a spontaneous and skilful restructuring of the situation in such a way that there will be no further disruption to the learning process: teachers restructure the power outcome in the classroom with a view to allowing learning to proceed without disruption.

So far we have seen some of the strategies a teacher may use to circumscribe the actions of small groups and individual children. But the communicative strategies we have observed are not confined to teachers, they are the normal communicative strategies which, for example, parents may use when talking to their children. Thinking about them, we might be led to ask ourselves: 'What is so special about that?' What is less obvious from this extract is that whilst teachers and parents may use the same communicative strategies with children, the context in which they operate is different.

In this extract we have looked at a few isolated examples, but we have to consider them in the context in which the teacher works. She does not simply circumscribe the actions of an individual child, or small group of children, as a parent might. She circumscribes the possibilities for the future actions of thirty children simultaneously and she does this continuously throughout the day. Whilst a parent may take time to talk to a child, unpressured by the demands of other children, this is not the case for the teacher. This extract of a teacher working in her classroom took place in less than seven minutes. What is obvious when watching the video is that the teacher has to be a fast, clear thinker. She has to have the ability to sum up situations in an instant, she has to know what kinds of power outcomes are possible and she has to know which power strategies are likely to achieve the power outcomes that she needs in order to get her work done. In short, the teacher has to have expert communication skills, skills which far exceed the demands of ordinary conversations.

What we can observe from this transcription is different teacher identities and different power strategies in operation. We can see the following:

- Dominant identities where the teacher limits the possibilities of future action for children.

- Less dominant identities where the teacher facilitates the possibilities of future action for the children.

But perhaps what is more important is the picture we gain of a teacher slipping rapidly from one identity to another. Gentle with Susie, firm and emphatic with Barry, then gently back to Susie. We see one rapid teacher identity after another, to enable her to cope with the demands of the different situations. But why did she change her identity?

Why did this teacher change her identity?

One of the reasons for a change in the teacher's identity may well have been the interpersonal dynamics in the classroom. For example, David was a very demanding child. He often disrupted the class and aggressively sought the teacher's attention. In this particular instance the teacher praised him for his efforts, but she did not devote much time to him individually, because he had already made great demands upon her time earlier in the day and did so again later. Susie was a very shy child and the teacher was trying to build up her confidence by praising and encouraging her. Barry and Peter, on the other hand, were both intelligent, boisterous individuals, who tended to become aggressive when they were left alone together for any length of time. If they were not handled firmly they could quickly disrupt the learning activities of the rest of the class.

A further reason which may have contributed to a change in the teacher's identity was the organisation. This teacher responds differently when she is teaching groups of children to when she is teaching individuals. If we compare the act of explaining to Emily with the act of explaining to Susie, we can see the differences in the teacher's identity. With Susie she was warm, friendly and able to devote her whole attention to a single child. Emily, however, was working with a group of children. Here the teacher had to cope with the competing demands of the other children in order to devote her attention to Emily, and this caused her to adopt a more dominant teacher identity.

In addition, the teacher responds in different ways according to the needs of different individuals. In her changes of identity she is trying to maximise the opportunities for learning for each child. But she has difficulty trying to do this equally for all of them. David, for example, sought her attention for a long time before she consented to go over and look at his work. She was too busy with Susie to attend to him, then as she moved away she saw a group of children who needed help. It was only when David touched her arm that she told the group in difficulties: 'All right. I'll just see to David because he was next, and then I will come to you.' We see the same thing when the interaction with Susie was interrupted by Peter and Barry:

> . . . Now I'm not going to talk to either of you, until I have finished with Susie. So you might as well go away . . . and put your hand up when you can see I have finished with Susie . . . And you can do the same because I am not talking to you until I have finished with Susie . . . Well you'll just have to wait . . . You'll just have to wait, won't you?

To a lesser extent we see the teacher balancing the needs of the different children in the group when she was talking to Emily: 'Shh-hh. Let her tell me. Let her tell me . . .' Later the teacher acknowledges, but does not take up Colin's suggestion:

> Colin: I thought you meant . . . she has . . . she had . . . she had a bit of er . . . She had two flats . . . and she put on something . . . but she took off more than she put on.
> Teacher: Mmm. (Nods to Colin, then turns to Emily.)

In short, what we begin to see is that the teacher is changing her identity in response to the power strategies that the children are operating upon her.

Some of the children's dominant power strategies in this and other extracts consist of the following:

- Interrupting the teacher.
- Fiddling whilst she is talking.
- Yawning.
- Not paying attention.
- Distracting the other children.
- Arguing with their peers and with the teacher.
- Refusing or failing to respond to the teacher's questions.
- Answering questions that have been asked of another child.

The children also use less dominant strategies with their teacher. In this particular example we can see the following:

- Nodding assent.
- Trying to explain.
- Requesting the teacher to look at their work.
- Smiling.
- Establishing eye contact with the teacher.
- Paying careful attention.
- Waiting until the teacher has finished what she is doing.
- Responding to humour.

- Politely seeking explanations when confused.
- Requesting permission to move to a more suitable working position.

Here again we can observe how the variety of less dominant strategies used by the children is far greater than the range of dominant strategies. We can also see the two-way operation of power. We can clearly see this negotiation of the learning context between the teacher and the children: it is a negotiation of what the children will allow the teacher to do and what the teacher will allow the children to do.

From these examples we can see how the teacher and the children make continuous demands on each other, and learning can only proceed with a substantial amount of co-operation from both the teacher and pupils. Here again, teacher identity is affected by the degree of co-operation between the teacher and pupils. Where there are continuous disruptions, as there had been earlier in the morning from Barry, Peter and David, the teacher will be obliged to assume a more dominant identity more frequently than in a class where the children were more co-operative. In a lesson where there were few disruptions and the learning was proceeding smoothly, the teacher would have greater freedom in selecting appropriate teacher identities with the pupils:

- The teacher's identity is affected by the competing demands made upon the teacher by the children.
- Teaching and learning requires a substantial amount of co-operation from both the teacher and the pupils.
- The teacher's identity is influenced by the degree of co-operation between the teacher and pupils.

When we examine the learning context in these terms, the notion of 'quality of learning' becomes far more complex. We can begin to see that the 'quality of learning' does not rest simply in the hands of the teacher, but also with the children: the quality of what is allowed to happen in the classroom is very much a negotiation between the teacher and the pupils.

Suggestions for teachers

1. Think about the last lesson you taught or the last lesson that you saw someone else teach. What are the most important things you remember? Make some notes about them.
2. How would these events affect the way you would handle the

power relationships in any future lessons with this group of children? Make a few notes about the changes you would make.

3. If you are working with other teachers share your notes with them. What power strategies would they have used in your situation? What power strategies would you have used in their situation?

4. Are the power strategies you would use the same or different from those of your colleagues? Which strategies would be the most appropriate?

4

Teaching styles: the balance of power

In the previous chapter we saw how the teacher and the children co-operated together to negotiate the learning experience. However, levels of co-operation between the teacher and the pupils can vary. When levels of co-operation between the teacher and the children are low, the children can make the job of the teacher more difficult. In the short extract which follows, the teacher in the previous chapter was explaining how to play the game with the Diennes apparatus:

Teacher: All the people doing this please . . . (*The children carry on.*) . . . Stop and listen . . . (*Matthew continues playing with the blocks.*) . . . Matthew . . . Stop and listen . . . (*Matthew continues. She puts her hands on his to stop him playing with the blocks. Marie approaches, needing attention. She stands by the teacher.*) STOP . . . and listen . . . (*He stops.*) Right, I'll just explain it again because we're having a bit of a problem with this. When you're near the end . . . you're almost ready to build your block . . . if you throw more than you need you CAN'T GO . . . You miss a go because you can't bust. You can't go over. All right? You have to wait until you get the right number which will not take you over the top . . . (*The child on her right is playing and not listening. She puts her hand on his head.*) Have you got that? (*She directs the question at the child who was playing. He says 'Yes'.*) So with this one you can't have more than? . . . What? . . . (*Silence, although the children did know the answer.*) You can't have more than what . . . (*Long silence.*) What do you need?
Tony: Six longs . . .
Teacher: Six longs . . . So if you throw any more than six longs . . . All right? You can't have more than you need to finish. That's what makes it quite difficult to finish. All right? Don't forget . . . Don't forget when it is someone else's turn you mustn't touch your blocks and things. You must let them have their turn because you should be listening to what they're saying. (*The children on her left and right are fiddling with the blocks. The next child along yawns and shuffles restlessly. The child standing by the teacher taps her arm, in an attempt to get her attention.*) . . . Can you not fiddle, because I haven't finished talking . . . Thank you . . . Matthew . . . (*He continues playing.*)

. . . When each person is having their turn, they must say what they are doing, and you must listen. That is very important. Right, Okay. Carry on then.

Here we see the children as a group using strategies which were less than co-operative. When the teacher says 'Stop and listen' They continue what they are doing. Matthew continues playing with the blocks even after several tellings and she places her hands over his to restrain him physically. Next, Marie approaches, needing attention. She stands by the teacher. They demand attention. Then she sees the child on her right, who is playing and not listening. She puts her hand on his head. They don't pay attention. After that, although the children did know the answer, they did not answer her questions. They avoid answering questions and taking an active part in the lesson. Then we see a whole range of unco-operative strategies:

(*The children on her left and right are fiddling with the blocks. The next child along yawns and shuffles restlessly. The child standing by the teacher taps her arm, in an attempt to get her attention.*) . . . Can you not fiddle, because I haven't finished talking . . . Thank you . . . Matthew . . . (*He continues playing.*) . . . When each person is having their turn, they must say what they are doing and you must listen. That is very important. Right, Okay. Carry on then.

- They fiddle and distract the other children.
- They yawn and show disinterest.
- They shuffle and become restless.
- They tap the teacher's arm to attract her attention.

This teacher handled the unco-operative strategies calmly and firmly, but not all teachers do this.

In another extract where a group of nine-year-old children were having a discussion about whether fish can feel, the teacher handled the situation differently. The discussion took place between Ben, Michael, Peter and their teacher. Ben was an aggressively intelligent child, who wanted to run the discussion himself. On several occasions it was necessary for the teacher to intervene when Ben produced unco-operative strategies, in order to allow the other children to contribute to the discussion. The teacher in this example had to work very hard just to keep the discussion going.

Perhaps the most interesting difference between this discussion and the earlier one was amongst the children themselves. In the first example of the class discussion the children were sharing the discourse structure of the discussion and taking group responsibility for what happened. At no point in the discussion did this happen. Eventually Ben and Peter began to argue about whether fish could, or could not feel. Peter insisted that they could feel and Ben, equally vehemently, insisted that they could not. At first Peter ignored Ben and directed his comments at the teacher: '. . . and Sir, if you tap the side of the tank, Sir, it swims away . . . it can feel it, Sir . . .' The teacher begins to work within the existing power relationships repeating what Peter has said, but Ben interrupted more insistently with a further challenge:

Teacher: You think that fish can feel . . .
Ben: They can't, Sir, they can't!

At this point the discussion has become an argument. The children are no longer listening to each other and are only interested in having their points accepted by the teacher. Here the teacher intervenes, but very hesitantly, and before he can do very much Peter interrupts again with a far better strategy. He resorts to calm reasonableness, supported by superior knowledge:

Teacher: Now . . . I think we have to . . .
Peter: Sir, they have a strip down their body . . . and Sir, they can feel through that . . .

The teacher, realising that this is likely to be the most effective solution, resorts to politeness to defuse the situation and asks Peter to repeat his point, thus re-establishing Peter and lending support to his comments. However, even this skilful variety of strategies failed to pacify Ben who, this time, challenges very petulantly: ' They can't!' At this point the teacher stepped in again. He adopted a very dominant position and a dominant power strategy. This time he resorts to the authority vested in him as the teacher and clearly indicates that the discussion will have to stop if the boys cannot be sensible.

Although we may attribute Ben's behaviour to youth and inexperience, his continually dominant and confrontational power strategies oblige the teacher to adopt dominant power strategies. In effect Ben's behaviour is obliging the teacher to take decisions that in other circumstances the teacher might not have chosen to make.

It is under this pressure that the teacher seems hesitant. He threatens to stop the discussion then, at the last minute, he changes his mind. He encourages the children to continue, but there is a long silence. None of the children are willing to co-operate and the discussion becomes a prolonged silence.

At this point the listener is under the impression that it would have been better if the teacher had not interfered here. The teacher had adopted a very dominant position to set aside Ben's point and support Peter's point, but he could not simply leave Ben in this state of dismissal. Such a strategy may have led to bitterness and further confrontation. Clearly the teacher is in a difficult position.

In previous examples we have seen how teachers avoid confrontations in the classroom, but should a confrontation arise there are a variety of power strategies that a teacher may choose from. The teacher may choose to:

- disengage from the situation;
- adopt weaker power strategies to 'defuse' the situation; or
- settle the question by displaying superior knowledge.

In this instance the teacher resorts to the dominant power strategy of displaying superior knowledge. In effect he rises to his full teacher height and demonstrates his superiority.

Given the lively nature of this group of children, it turned out that the teacher may not have selected the most effective power strategies in this particular situation. The teacher has been operating in a very dominant position in the discussion. At this point none of the children initiate another exchange. There is a long silence and unless the teacher himself generates a new exchange the discussion will come to an end.

To some extent the children are now dependent upon the teacher for the continuation of the lesson. In short, as a result of the dominant power relationship which the teacher has generated within the group, he has placed himself, wittingly or unwittingly, in the position of leader of the discussion.

Here we gain a glimpse of the skilful nature of teaching and how easy it can be to make a mistake in the management of the power relationships between the teacher and pupils. The power strategies used by a teacher with one group of children may be perfectly effective, but completely ineffective with a different group of children, depending on the degree of co-operation between the teacher and pupils.

In comparison with the other teacher holding a class discussion in Chapter 2, this was clearly a very different experience. Both teachers and both sets of children behaved in very different ways. How can we explain these differences? Perhaps the most revealing place to start is with the teachers' power strategies.

A comparison of the teachers' power strategies

The teacher in Chapter 2 had placed the children's chairs in a circle, the teacher in this chapter had also placed the children in a circle, but they were in a circle around a table. In both examples the teachers selected the child who was going to make the next contribution. However, this became less frequent during the confrontations of the discussion about fish. In this example the teacher at times lost control of the organisation, but apart from this we see very little difference in the organisation of the lesson.

In the discussion about the brain (p.9) the teacher did not choose the topic of discussion, did not contribute to the discussion and the children took this responsibility upon themselves. In the discussion about the fish (p.31) the teacher had chosen the topic for discussion, the teacher actually took part in the discussion and was at times forced to lead it. He attempted to direct the progress of the discussion by asking leading questions at critical moments. Here the children did not take responsibility for the discussion themselves, but relied on the direction of their teacher. At no point did they take responsibility amongst themselves as a group for the discussion. They merely responded to the opportunities that the teacher created for them.

The differing ages of the children must also be taken into account. We might have expected to find differences in the kinds of discussion that teachers might hold with nine-year-old children and with six-year-old children (p.9). It might have been expected for example, that older children might have been more able to select their own topic for discussion and take greater responsibility for the discussion themselves. Interestingly, this did not happen. To the contrary, it was the younger children who chose their own topic for discussion and took greater responsibility for the direction of the discussion.

If we compare this teacher's identity with that of the teacher leading the discussion on the brain (p.9), we can begin to see that whilst the latter teacher adopted less dominant power strategies with her pupils, the former teacher adopted more dominant power strategies with his pupils. Further recordings of this teacher in fact seemed to indicate that he habitually adopted dominant power strategies and that this was his prevalent teaching style. Inevitably these teacher preferences resulted in a generally more dominant teacher identity in the classroom and subsequent differences in the teacher's power strategies. In turn it affected the power strategies which the children operated upon the teacher, sometimes creating more power management difficulties than may have been necessary.

In order to control the situation in her classroom the teacher of the six-year-olds (p.9) only helped children who lost track of what they were saying. She encouraged with long eye contact and verbal encouragement and the children began to take on the responsibility for the discussion themselves. They demonstrated very effectively that even at the very young age of six they were quite capable of holding a serious discussion with a little encouragement from the teacher.

The teacher in the second discussion (p.31) adopted a dominant teacher identity and habitually dominant power strategies, which allow us to pinpoint differences in the styles of teaching of the two teachers. We saw the second teacher:

- Restraining contributions from some children and encouraging contributions from others.
- Using direct questioning to oblige children to develop their points.
- Being hesitant in knowing how to respond.
- Defusing a confrontation by demonstrating superior knowledge.
- Establishing a consensus of accepted knowledge within the group – then leaving it open to challenge.
- Placing himself in the position of having to lead the discussion.

What we begin to see from these differences in the way the second teacher structured the possibilities for the future actions of his pupils is that in adopting a very dominant teacher identity and dominant power strategies, right from the start, this teacher moved from one difficult situation to another. As the discussion developed the problems increased and the children learnt correspondingly less as each difficulty was dealt with in a yet more dominant manner, which in turn led to even greater competition to gain the approval of the teacher.

There are several important lessons to be learnt from this comparison. The first and most interesting is a comment on the response of the children. The identity which the teacher adopts in the classroom has a direct effect on the interaction, which in turn affects the possible responses that the children can make. This point is illustrated very clearly in these two examples (pp.9, 31). Where the teacher was calm, apparently unassuming and very reasonable, the children emulated her example. In effect, by her example she fostered consideration, a sense of mutual respect and justice amongst her pupils. She came very close to setting a good example of equality and this could be seen in the respect which the pupils demonstrated for each other in their contributions to the discussion. Because the children were trusted by their teacher they were not afraid to take initiatives and the teacher never found herself in the position of having to lead the discussion. This was particularly important, because it effectively made the pupils independent of their teacher and enabled them to take responsibility for the discussion upon themselves.

On the other hand, adopting a habitually dominant identity and dominant power strategies had quite a different effect on the second group of children (p.31). The teacher's dominant power strategies created inequality. The children found that only one person at a time could be dominant and they had to compete with each other and the teacher if they wanted to take part in the discussion. As a direct consequence of the inequality, confrontations arose, which led to the teacher escalating his own dominance in order to control the situation with yet more dominant power strategies. This in effect further escalated the competition to the point where the children were more concerned with competing with each other than they were with learning about fish.

Clearly it would be a mistake to generalise too far from these examples. Teachers frequently encounter children who will respond only to dominance. But it also is the case that in many instances where there is a sudden and unanticipated disruption to the lesson that the children are responding to the competitive compulsion of dominant power strategies.

From the comparison of these teachers holding discussions with their classes, the following become more evident:

- Teacher identity is demonstrated in the classroom in terms of the position the teacher adopts with the pupils. It is acted out in terms of habitual dominance or lack of dominance.
- Teacher identity is demonstrated in the kinds of power strategies the teacher uses. It is acted out in terms of the teacher's habitual use of dominant or less dominant power strategies.
- One of the ways in which teaching styles can be described is in terms of the power strategies that individual teachers habitually use.

In short, it is important that teachers recognise the importance of their teacher identity and the power strategies which they habitually use in the classroom. The habitual power strategies which a teacher uses can restrict or open up the learning possibilities for those who are being taught. For all teachers it is important to recognise the effects that their power strategies are likely to have upon the children, both in a group and as individuals.

Further, whilst all teachers must adopt dominant power strategies on occasions in their classrooms, it is important to be conscious of the positive effects of habitually less dominant power strategies which

- foster trust, confidence and security;
- encourage in children a sense of self-worth and respect for others;
- encourage independence and self-reliance;
- encourage children to develop their own initiatives; and

- foster a sense of equality.

On the other hand, whilst habitual dominance may not prevent children from learning, it is possible that habitually dominant power strategies may carry with them certain inherent risks. It is possible that they may

- foster competition to the point of confrontation;
- damage group and individual relationships;
- discourage the children from taking initiatives;
- make the children dependent upon their teacher; and
- risk damaging the child's future attitude towards teachers and education.

At this point we can really begin to see the importance of the relationship between 'who the teacher is' in the classroom and what he or she can achieve with his or her pupils. The teacher's identity and power strategies effectively limit, or create possibilities for 'who the children can be'. They affect the child's self-image and self-esteem. But these differences should not lead us into thinking that there are right and wrong ways of managing the power relationships in the classroom. What these two examples of teachers holding discussions with children in their classrooms illustrate is that

- teachers have choices about the way they handle situations; and
- sometimes these choices can be difficult.

But this choice is not unlimited, for example:

- If the teacher adopts an identity and power strategies which are not sufficiently dominant, he or she will lose control of the learning situation.
- But conversely, if the teacher adopts an identity and power strategies which are too dominant, then again, he or she will cause confrontations, which may also lead to loss of control of the learning situation.
- The teacher's professional skill involves the ability to manage the power relationships in the classroom effectively.
- Effective teachers understand the benefits to be gained by adopting both dominant and less dominant power strategies in specific situations. They also understand that there are limits beyond which they must not go if they do not wish to lose control of the learning situation.

Here we gain yet another insight into the professional skills of teachers:

- The teacher's professional skill involves the ability to know when the greatest effects can be achieved by setting up dominant or less dominant power relationships.
- The teacher's professional skill involves the ability to recognise the upper and lower limits of dominant and less dominant power strategies.

Suggestions for teachers

1. Try to record a lesson that you have taught, or think carefully about the last lesson that you remember teaching. What were your main professional concerns? How did this affect what you did in the classroom?
2. Think about your teacher identity. Are you a teacher who habitually uses dominant or less dominant power strategies? What changes could you make to develop or improve this aspect of your work?
3. Can you find an example in your lesson of the children taking responsibility for the learning? If not, how could you change your lesson to encourage this in future? If there are examples of the children taking responsibility for what happens, how could you further develop this in the future?
4. Do all of the children in your class share responsibility for what happens, or is this responsibility shared only by the most outgoing children? How could you ensure that all of the children share this responsibility?

5

When teachers use the media: power failure

So far we have looked at the skills teachers use to manage the power relationships in their classroom. We have seen how teaching is very much about using effective power strategies to ensure that the learning proceeds smoothly. However, there are occasions when teachers do not manage the learning situations of their pupils, for example, when a television or radio broadcast is used. What happens when the teacher is not in control of the power relationships in the learning situation? The extract which follows is a transcription of part of a movement programme for reception class children. (The transcription is from *Playtime* by Hazel Glynne, a BBC radio programme for schools, which was produced in the second stage of the research.)

(*Introductory theme music.*)
John: Hello. I'm John.
Susan: And I'm Susan. Hello. Have you ever looked at the different buildings around us?
Buildings are a great surprise.
Everyone's a different size.
Offices grow long and high,
Tall enough to touch the sky.
Houses seem more like a box,
Made of glue and building blocks.
Every time you look you see
Buildings shaped quite differently.
John: Perhaps you have watched some buildings being built near you, some shops or houses, or a tall block of flats.
Susan: Building sites can be really messy places, full of squelchy mud and puddles of water.
John: Ah, that doesn't worry me, because
I like mud.
I like it on my clothes,
I like it on my fingers,
I like it on my toes.

Dirt is pretty ordinary,
And dust is a dud.
For a real big mess up
I like mud.
(*Repeats the verse.*)

After these introductory comments, the activities for the children begin:

Susan: Mud's fun, but it is very messy.
John: We're going for a walk in the mud now. So put on your boots. One foot
. . . (*Boot putting-on noise.*) Then the other foot . . . (*Boot putting-on noise.*)
Now, we're ready for our walk. Stand up . . . (*Standing-up music.*) I can see a
building site over there. Let's go and see what's happening.
Susan: Get ready to lift your knees up high as you squelch through the sticky
thick mud.
John: You'll have to move quite slowly so you don't slip over. Off you go then.
Slowly and carefully. (*Mud-walking music.*)
Susan: And stand still. Look John, can you see that puddle?
John: Oh yes. Do you like splashing in puddles? Let's run and jump in that big
puddle to clean off the mud on our Wellingtons. Ready? Come on! (*Puddle-
splashing music.*)
Susan: Let's have one more huge, big splash. Don't fall in. Get ready to run
and . . . splash! (*Running and splashing music.*)

At this point the programme turns its attention to what is happening
on the building site:

John: We have reached the building site at last . . . I wonder if you can guess
what the different sounds are by listening? Listen carefully. What do you
think is happening? (*Tapping and scraping noise.*)
Susan: Well, I can hear bricks being moved, and that sounds as if something
is being scraped on to the bricks.
John: That's right. It's cement. You put cement on the bricks, and build them
up on top of each other. When the cement dries it goes very hard, and the
bricks can't fall down.

This activity of listening and guessing is then repeated with another
sound:

Susan: Here's another building site noise. Can you guess what this is?
(*Sawing sound.*) Do you know? Someone's sawing up the wood. (*Hammering
sound.*) . . . And they're nailing the shorter lengths together to make a window frame.

Having introduced some of the main activities on the building site,
the children are then invited to try for themselves:

John: There's lots of work to do on a building site. And you can help. Stand up
and find a space. (*Space-finding music.*) We are going to do some building
first. You'll have to pick up the bricks one at a time, and carefully, build up
the wall. Start low down, near the ground. And slowly build the wall higher and

higher. Ready? (*Wall-building music.*) The wall's half built. Let's stack some bricks on the top and build the wall even higher. Ready? (*Wall-building music.*) A-A-And stop. (*Long drawn-out 'and'.*) The wall's built now. So let's make the window frames. Window frames are made of wood. Pick up the plank of wood in front of you. Pick up the saw. And get ready to push and pull your saw backwards and forwards to make the window frames. Ready? (*Sawing music.*) Put your saw down. A-A-And stop.

Susan: All we've got to do now is hammer the pieces of wood together. Get ready with your hammer and nails, and try not to bang your fingers. (*Humorously.*) Ready then? (*Hammering music.*) And stand still again. I think you've all worked really hard today . . . So come and sit where you can hear clearly . . . (*Sitting-where-you-can-hear-clearly music, followed by the story.*)

This broadcast lesson is accompanied by notes for teachers suggesting ways in which teachers may prepare children for the broadcast and follow-up activities after the broadcast. This interlude is very pleasant to listen to and is of a kind that is usually very much enjoyed by young children. It has the advantage of introducing new voices into the classroom. It can also draw on resources such as a whole band of musicians and interesting sound effects, which are often beyond the teacher's normal range of resources. However, enjoyable as it might be, how does it differ from teaching in a classroom?

One of the most striking observations to be made about this extract is its tight structure. Throughout the broadcast the children are expected to sit and listen, stand up, move carefully, etc. The distance between the presenters and the children, who have never met and cannot see each other, requires that the children are given very explicit instructions about what is coming next and what they are expected to do. At no point can the children effectively take part in this discourse. They are expected only to do as they are told.

We saw a similar example of this situation in the second extract (p.00) where the teacher dismissed the children from her class at break time and lunch time. That example was characterised by ritual language and contrasts in the loudness and softness of the teacher's voice. In this extract too, there are examples of ritual language. For example, John says: 'Now, we're ready for our walk. Stand up . . . (*Standing-up music.*)' He tells the children what is about to happen, then uses the ritual signal 'Stand up' which all of the children recognise as a sign that the activity is about to begin. Interestingly the signal is reinforced with music. Every time the children are told to 'Stand up' the same few bars of music are played. Similarly, Susan brings the activity to an end with an equally recognisable signal: 'And stand still.'

Later John gives the same signal for the activity to cease, but interestingly he uses his voice to reinforce the actual words:

A-A-And stop. (*Long drawn out 'and'.*) The wall's built now. So let's make the window frames. Window frames are made of wood. Pick up the plank of wood in front of you. Pick up the saw. And get ready to push and pull your saw backwards and forwards to make the window frames. Ready? (*Sawing music.*) Put your saw down. A-A-And stop.

The long drawn out 'A-A-And stop' gives the children plenty of warning that the stop signal is coming. Just as the teacher in the second example (p.5) dismissed her class by using her voice in contrasting ways, so this radio presenter also uses his voice. This particular contribution of John's is interesting because it also contains other *ritual* signals. For example, he uses repetition: 'Pick up the plank of wood in front of you. Pick up the saw.'

This repetition, unlike the other examples of repetition we have examined, where teachers were manipulating the discourse structure creates redundancy in the language. It is much easier for the children to predict what is going to happen next if the same language patterns are repeated. In a situation where the participants do not know and cannot see each other, this is of great assistance to the children. In short, this redundancy is necessary for the smooth procedure of a situation where the participants cannot see each other. For this reason we can also appreciate the necessity of a warning that a particular signal is coming, for example, John uses a warning then the signal to start the activity: 'And get ready . . . Ready?'

The activity also ends with a warning and then the anticipated signal: 'Put your saw down. A-A-And stop.' There are many examples of this tightly structured use of repetition and ritual signals. In fact, we soon begin to realise that there is far more use of this technique in the radio broadcast than when the teacher dismissed her class.

The highly structured language is also complemented by the structure of the activity. This broadcast can only suggest activities for children to do and expect them to perform the prescribed tasks. This is very limiting in comparison with a movement lesson taken by a teacher, who is likely to praise the children for their efforts, encourage them to try harder and allow opportunities for practice where the children may not have performed as well as might be expected. Teachers might also have used individual children to demonstrate and stimulate the other children to make greater efforts. None of this can happen in the radio broadcast.

Further, in a broadcast 'lesson' there is no opportunity to look at the creative efforts of individual children. In order to do this the teacher would need to pre-record the programme and switch off the tape during the lesson in order to create these learning opportunities.

In practice this is how many teachers use broadcasts of this kind, but it is not always easy to find the best point at which to switch off the tape recorder owing to the tight structure of the broadcast. And finally, wherever the teacher chooses to switch off the tape there is an inevitable disruption in the lesson owing to the tightly structured sequence of the broadcast.

Furthermore, the language itself is quite unlike the lively dynamic and spontaneous language used by the teachers in the previous extracts. On the contrary, the language of this broadcast is stilted and artificial. For example, the extract begins: '*John:* Hello. I'm John./*Susan:* And I'm Susan. Hello.' For young children it may seem strange that the teacher starts the lesson by saying 'hello' and announcing their first names. Most teachers are known as Mrs X or Mr Y and are more likely to introduce themselves with: 'Good morning (Hello), my name is Mrs X, and today I am going to . . .' Teachers' introductions do not normally encourage the children to respond and it seems unusual in a situation where the radio presenters and the children cannot hear each other to adopt this form of greeting.

Right from the start it is clear to the children that these voices are not the voices of 'teachers', because they do not behave in the same way that teachers behave. We can see similar differences in:

John: . . . I wonder if you can guess what the different sounds are by listening? Listen carefully. What do you think is happening? (*Tapping and scraping noise.*)
Susan: Well, I can hear bricks being moved, and that sounds as if something is being scraped on to the bricks.
John: That's right. It's cement. You put cement on the bricks, and build them up on top of each other. When the cement dries it goes very hard, and the bricks can't fall down.

Whilst the children may willingly accept this situation, they know that this is not the way their teacher normally behaves. When John says 'I wonder if you can guess what the different sounds are by listening?' we have to assume that this question is directed at the children, after all it is not the kind of question that adults would normally ask each other. The assumption that this question is addressed to the children seems to be confirmed in John's next phrase: 'Listen carefully. What do you think is happening?' This is hardly the kind of language that we would expect adults to use to each other. Thus we are led to interpret this interaction as an interaction between the children and the presenters. However, the children, although they may answer the question, cannot be heard by the presenters and this creates a problem. Without a reply to the question the discourse structure will be incomplete. John presents a situation and a problem in '. . . I wonder if you can guess what the different sounds are by listening? Listen carefully. What do you think is happening? (*Tapping and scraping noise.*)' The broadcast would sound very stilted if there was a long silence at this point for the children to answer the question before the presenter continued with a new situation and problem.

In order to make the language appear as natural as possible it is essential for someone to answer the question before the 'conversation' can continue. Susan, the other presenter, provides the answer in: 'Well, I can hear bricks being moved, and that sounds as if something is being scraped on to the bricks.' John then completes the discourse structure with an evaluation: 'That's right. It's cement. You put cement on the bricks, and build them up on top of each other. When the cement dries it goes very hard, and the bricks can't fall down.' This solves the problem of the completion of the discourse structure, but it is a contrived situation, which lacks spontaneity.

In an ordinary lesson, if the teacher had asked this question, the children would have answered it. The fact that the children are unable to answer it creates an extra problem in that, as Susan provides a solution and John provides the evaluation, we have a conversation aimed at the children, which is being held between the presenters. The artificiality arises when two adults are heard to hold a conversation suitable for children. We see this happen again in:

> *Susan:* . . . Look John, can you see that puddle?
> *John:* Oh yes. Do you like splashing in puddles? Let's run and jump in that big puddle to clean off the mud on our Wellingtons. Ready? Come on! (*Puddle-splashing music.*)'

Here the presenters actually direct the conversation at each other and they might well have just been talking to each other, except some adults may find it surprising to hear other adults talking about splashing in puddles. The concluding comment in this sequence provides more than a suspicion that the 'conversation' is aimed at the children: '*Susan:* Let's have one more huge, big splash. Don't fall in. Get ready to run and . . . splash! (*Running and splashing music.*)'

Here again, we can sense a slight confusion about who is supposed to be saying what to whom. The presenters seem to slip uneasily from having a conversation between themselves, to attempting to have a conversation in which their young listeners are expected to participate. This difficulty is often sensed by the children. It is not uncommon for a child to shout out the answer to a broadcaster's question, then shrink in embarrassment when the other presenter answers the question, thus making it seem as if the child has made a mistake and misinterpreted the presenter's intentions.

A further difficulty arises because the children and the presenters cannot see each other, they do not have a shared context. For this reason the presenters have to provide information about the context. For example both John and Susan provide contextual information in:

> *John:* We have reached the building site at last.
> *Susan:* And I am quite tired after that splashing and squelching. Let's go and sit down on that patch of dry grass over there.

Statements such as 'We have reached the building site at last' are not common in spoken conversations. The participants in any spoken conversation would all be able to see for themselves that they had reached the building site, and would be less likely to comment on it. Therefore this would be a very unnatural statement to make in a normal conversation. It is yet another indicator that this is far from a 'normal conversation' and it contributes to the apparent artificiality in the language of this broadcast.

As we have seen in previous examples, the language we have looked at was generated by a social context, therefore if artificiality was reflected in the language of this broadcast, it is almost certainly reflecting the artificiality of the social situation. Inevitably this begs the question about the artificiality of the teaching situation in a broadcast lesson. This must lead us to ask: 'In what ways was this an artificial teaching situation?' Perhaps the most useful approach to this question is to think about the power strategies of the presenters.

The presenters' power strategies

Throughout the broadcast the presenters refer to each other as John and Susan, me, you or I and they directly address the children as you:

> *John:* Ah, that doesn't worry me, because
> I like mud.
> I like it on my clothes,
> I like it on my fingers,
> I like it on my toes.
> Dirt is pretty ordinary,
> And dust is a dud.
> For a real big mess up
> I like mud.

The children are included in the 'conversation' and the activities at a very early stage. '*Susan:* Mud's fun, but it is very messy./*John:* We're going for a walk in the mud now. So put on your boots.' However, this inclusion is sometimes a very uncomfortable and artificial inclusion. In spite of the tight structure of the broadcast, there are many occasions when the children experience confusion about whether or not they are expected to respond and when they are expected to do this.

In two places there are attempts to make interpersonal contact with the children by making 'humorous' comments. We can see this in: '*Susan:* Let's have one more huge, big splash. Don't fall in. Get ready to run and . . . splash! (*Running and splashing music.*)' and '*Susan:* All we've got to do now is hammer the pieces of wood together. Get ready with your hammer and nails and try not to bang your fingers. (*Humorously.*)' But the humour of the latter comment may well have been lost on certain children who were not sure about how to use a hammer, so it is of limited value.

The presenters' power strategies can be summed up in a very short list of instructions: 'Stand up . . . Get ready to . . . Off you go then. And stand still . . . Ready? . . . Listen carefully . . . Stand up and find a space . . . A-A-And stop . . . So come and sit where you can hear clearly . . .' If we compare these strategies with those of the teacher in previous examples they are extremely limited. If a teacher had taken this lesson he or she would have spent a considerable amount of time helping the children to develop their spatial awareness, by insisting that they found their own spaces and did not bump into each other. The teacher would have made sure that the room was large enough for the number of children carrying out the activity. During the lesson he or she would have been monitoring and assessing the children's performance, allowing extra practice where necessary. The teacher would have evaluated the children's performance and given them feedback about it. In this broadcast there is an attempt at giving the children feedback: ' . . . I think you've all worked really hard today./*John:* Building a new house is hard work.' But it seems particularly artificial in a situation where the presenters could not see what the children had achieved and on a difficult day in school, when perhaps the children were more excitable than usual, it is conceivable that it would be totally inappropriate!

Immediately an interesting situation presents itself. The radio presenters, who do not know the children and have never visited the building in which the lesson is taking place, are not in a position to construct a teaching identity. They cannot assess the power situation or adopt appropriate power strategies, because they do not possess the knowledge which teachers possess when they are teaching. This naturally creates difficulties.

In the previous examples we saw how teachers structured the possibilities for future actions of their pupils by:

- Setting up different kinds of power relationships with different individuals.
- Assessing the state of play in the discourse.
- Assessing the most effective point of entry into the discourse.
- Manipulating the structure of the discourse.
- Operating within the constraints of the discourse.
- Restructuring the power relationships.
- Inhibiting contributions from some pupils.
- Encouraging contributions from other pupils.
- Continually re-establishing the state of consent and co-operation between the teacher and pupils.
- Using ritual language.
- Using routine sequences to control large groups.
- Using contrasts in the loudness and softness of his or her voice.
- Using dominant rising tones.
- Using body language to control attempts at contesting the power outcome.
- Using strategies of disengagement.

In this broadcast how many of these power strategies were present? We noted the use of ritual language and the use of routine sequences to control the activities. At one point John also used his voice to control the activity, but beyond this there were no real attempts to vary the power strategies. It is of course hardly surprising that none of these strategies were present in the broadcast because the presenters could not see or hear the children. They simply were not in a position to structure the power outcome of the situation and have to rely heavily upon the class teacher to do this. They could not adequately control the learning experiences of the children and were not in a position to create new opportunities for learning.

In effect, without the assistance of the class teacher, it is unlikely that a 'lesson' of this kind would be successful. But in fairness, the producers of this programme did not intend it as a teaching activity. This fact is underlined by the fact that the programme is accompanied by notes with suggestions for discussion before the programme and activities after it, which teachers may like to incorporate into their teaching.

This programme is simply a set of instructions for activities for groups of children and was never intended to be a teaching activity. It is the equivalent of an audio workcard, which teachers may incorporate into their teaching, but it is a very useful audio workcard because it helps us to understand that

- there is a difference between teaching and instructing; and

- the difference between this set of activity instructions and a teaching activity is the teacher's identity and his or her variety of power strategies.

What we can begin to grasp from this discussion is that

- the essential qualities which distinguish a teaching activity from any other related activities are the teacher's identity and his or her effective power strategies.

Without a teacher identity and a variety of effective power strategies an activity cannot be considered to be a teaching activity.

Suggestions for teachers

1. Choose a recorded radio or television broadcast aimed at the age group which you are currently teaching. Listen to it or watch it carefully all of the way through. Select the most interesting ten minutes for detailed consideration. Make a few notes on your reasons for selecting this particular few minutes.
2. What evidence can you find about the presenter's power strategies? Do the presenter's power strategies create any problems? Make a few notes on the difficulties you can pick out. How far does the presenter rely on the teacher for power strategies?
3. How would you describe the presenter's power strategies?
4. If you are working with other teachers or students, share your findings. Are they similar or different?
5. Try the same activities using a set of printed learning materials. What kinds of problems do they create for the writer? What kinds of problems do they create for the learner?
6. Try the same activities using a computer program designed to assist the learning of a particular concept. What kinds of problems does it create for the programmer? What kinds of problems does it create for the learner?

6

What do teachers do beyond their work in the classroom? Power in the staffroom

If we are genuinely trying to describe what primary teachers do, it is important to consider what teachers do beyond their work in the classroom with children. For example, teachers hold meetings where teaching teams discuss the overall plans for a particular group of children. Whole school staffs attend meetings to discuss school policies. Teachers also attend in-service courses and conferences. These activities are all considered to be part of the work of being a teacher, and we must ask ourselves: What part do these activities play in the work of a teacher?

In the extract which follows a teaching team of three primary teachers who work in a large primary school with parallel classes of eight-year-olds are meeting to discuss the topic of 'The Victorians' which they will be carrying out with their respective classes during the next term. The names have been changed to preserve anonymity. The teachers of these classes work closely together, sometimes mixing the classes and team teaching, sometimes taking their own classes in their own home base. This conversation was part of a teacher planning meeting to discuss the coming term's work. Present were Helen, Dianne and Fiona.

On first listening, this conversation seemed to wander and lack purpose. The teachers' talk ranged over a wide area of important aspects of planning their topic, but during this meeting they do not seem to reach any firm decisions. The conversation ranged unpredictably over

- how to get the topic started;
- the language curriculum;
- the National Curriculum;
- the maths curriculum;
- the science curriculum;

- concerns about children's learning (highlighting their individuality and inventiveness);
- resources that the children could be asked to bring in;
- an art activity;
- organising the project to get the maximum learning benefits;
- planning and questioning; and
- the balance of learning between skills and knowledge.

The later part of the conversation concerned itself with the problems of integrating and providing appropriate help for children with special needs. Although this may seem to have been a rambling discussion, there is a certain logic about it. For example, at one point Dianne says: 'How can we make sure that we get everything we need to get out of it? What about the organisation, I mean . . .?' One of the teachers' main concerns is related to organisation. Further references were made to aspects of the organisation when Helen said: 'We need to plan it carefully . . . think about the questions we set them . . . they have to be open ended . . . we have to make sure that the questions we set can be answered by the children . . .' Dianne was also concerned about the resources that the children would need to bring in: 'What kind of things do we need to ask them to bring . . . what do we need? We might get some clothes . . . I've got a christening gown . . .'

Throughout the conversation there are many and varied references to the knowledge that the children will be learning. Right from the earliest stages of the conversation, the knowledge that the children would learn had occupied a prominent place in the teachers' thinking. In a considerable stretch of conversation the teachers range over some of the knowledge that they hope will come out of their topic:

> *Dianne:* So really you're using them for talk . . . (*the things that the children will bring in*) communication skills . . .
> *Fiona:* Yes . . .
> *Dianne:* Language skills . . . the language curriculum . . .
> *Fiona:* Yes . . . that's it . . .
> *Helen:* Yeah, we have to go right the way across the National Curriculum.
> *Fiona:* Yes we can manage that . . . like maths we could look at Victorian games . . . counting, jumping . . . you know, . . . jumping squares, moving spaces . . . that would bring maths into it . . .
> *Dianne:* . . . Right . . .
> *Helen:* So how do you do the science part of the curriculum?

Naturally the core subjects in the National Curriculum were central to the teachers' concerns about knowledge, but there is evidence that at a later stage the foundation subjects will also receive due consideration. Fiona indicates her historical concerns when she says: 'Well we could look at children and how they spent their days in the past . . . I mean schools . . .you know . . . and factories . . .' and her concerns for art in: 'Yeah, well erm . . . We could start with an art activity . . . like Victorian cards (*Laughs.*) . . . Well, I mean . . . it will be so near to Christmas!/ *Helen:* Yeah! Why not! (*Laughs again.*)'

Already at this early stage in their discussions of the new topic we can see how this teaching team is beginning to explore the different considerations that must be taken into account before the teachers will take the next step of detailed planning. What is particularly interesting about this conversation is the range of issues that the teachers are bringing to bear on their decision-making process. Not only are they drawing together issues of organisation, interpersonal relationships and the knowledge that the children will learn, but there are also the legal requirements of their work.

We also see practical considerations when Fiona says:

Fiona: . . . Tell us a bit about your christening gown . . . How would you use it?
Dianne: Oh, in lots of different ways. I'd start off by asking the children if they knew what it was . . . and if they had anything at home like that . . .

There are considerations about learning theory when Helen says: 'But how d'you keep the balance between skills and process . . . what I call the doing learning . . . and knowing learning . . .?' What we begin to see from this discussion is that the teachers are considering and synthesising a very wide range of issues and knowledge in order to make their teaching plans – teachers synthesise a wide range of issues before they can make teaching plans.

However, in bringing together this wide range of issues, we can also see that teachers use language which would only be used in an educational context. There is talk of the National Curriculum, the science curriculum, the maths curriculum, language skills, communication skills, organisation, planning, open and closed questions. In other parts of the transcript there are references to 'drawing it out of the children', thinking time, less able children, children who are not learning in their first language, differentiation, acquiring, developing and applying skills, observing, hypothesising, predicting, recording, assessment and monitoring progress.

In order to be able to discuss and carry out their professional functions teachers have to know and use the professional references in which these issues are couched. Here we can begin to see how:

teachers have to be literate in the language of their profession in order to carry out their work.

In this discussion we can also see how this common professional language allows teachers to share their knowledge about their work. Sharing knowledge is important because teachers may have very different kinds of experience and expertise. This sharing of a common professional language with other professionals is important not only because it allows teachers to discuss issues relevant to their work and share knowledge in different areas of expertise, but the language itself also formulates which issues are relevant and which are not. This is particularly evident when Dianne begins talking about organisation: 'How can we make sure that we get all this out of it? What about the organisation, I mean . . . ? We will have to organise it so we don't tell the children everything they need to know . . . or that we think they need to know.' Here Dianne has raised questions of professional attitude and opinion. For example, not all teachers might agree that they should not tell children everything that they need to know. Underlying this statement is the professional belief that knowledge which children find out and understand for themselves is likely to be far more useful than knowledge which someone else has tried to tell them. It is as if Dianne is 'testing the water' with her fellow professionals. In Helen's contribution we see that the view is not contested. There is a consensus; Fiona steps in and reaffirms Helen's points: 'Yes, it doesn't happen by chance . . . They have to tell you . . .' This is followed by an affirmation from Helen: 'Yeah, it's sort of . . . pulled out of the children.' Now that all of the group have agreed that these values are acceptable to all of them, the next series of values and attitudes are raised when Dianne asks: 'So what sort of plans should we make?' Helen returns to her point about closed and open questions: 'Well it's gotta be open-ended questions we set . . . I mean, not closed ones . . .' But Fiona develops the thinking further with a point about how much time the children will need to carry out this work: 'What about the time they need to think . . .? I think that's important to be planned in . . . it's no good rushing through it . . . you can't hurry learning up . . . they need time . . .' And this is further developed by Helen: 'Yeah, the time that we're going to allow especially for those who aren't learning in their first language . . .'

During this stretch of the conversation the teachers are formulating their beliefs and values about the ways in which the work should be carried out. We see them raise important questions, formulating the ways which they as a group feel are the best methods of encouraging learning. Fortunately, amongst this group there is a great deal of consensus, but in larger groups it is possible that these issues would be contentious. Where contention exists the power relationship would be important: teachers influence the beliefs and values of their fellow professionals.

Meetings of this kind define the immediate context in which teachers carry out their work, so to some extent we can see that teachers influence the work of other teachers with whom they work: teachers define the immediate context in which their work and the work of their fellow professionals, will be carried out.

This may seem a very obvious and innocuous statement, but it carries with it important implications for the work of a teacher. It is important because it raises questions of respect for others and professional credibility. Clearly no self-respecting teacher would allow his or her professional context to be structured by the actions of any who were not held in the highest professional esteem and it is therefore not surprising that time and time again in the transcriptions contained in these chapters we can find examples of teachers establishing and re-establishing their professional credibility.

Although the discussion in this transcription was the friendliest, most humorous and supportive discussion, we should not be surprised to find challenges to the professional credibility of individuals. Perhaps one of the most obvious challenges in this discussion came when Fiona said:

> *Dianne:* What sort of things d'you think they should get out of 'The Victorians'?
> *Fiona:* Well . . . they'll learn about how people lived in the past . . . especially the children . . .
> *Helen:* M-m-m-m . . . d'you think we should focus on the children . . . or would it be better to have a wider span?

Dianne then adopts a dominant power strategy. She challenges the assumption that 'children' should be a focus for this topic: 'Not just children! I mean . . . we need to do more than that . . . ?' Fiona steps in with an explanation, an even more dominant strategy, to defend her professional actions: 'Well no . . . I think there's a lot in 'children' . . . I mean . . . there'll be more than enough for us to cover . . . (*Laughs.*)' At this point Dianne has a choice of raising the state of confrontation or capitulating. Adopting even more dominant strategies at this point may lead to conflict and confrontation. Sensibly Dianne accepts Fiona's explanation and the discussion is allowed to continue. She simply signals her consent with: 'Yeah.'

In another stretch of the conversation we see a very interesting challenge towards the end of the discussion when Helen asks: 'But how d'you keep the balance between this topic and all the other things we have to do . . .?' This is a direct challenge to the professional knowledge of the other teachers present and it is expressed in a dominant power strategy. For the other participants there can be no evading the issue. The responses are very interesting. Dianne successfully attempts to pass the challenge on to Fiona. With a laugh she says: 'Fiona's better at that than me!' But in doing so she damages her professional credibility within the group. Recognising this Fiona attempts to restore the situation with: 'I'm not really!' In effect she says: 'That was only a joke, Dianne really didn't mean that . . .' The laughter creates a break in the discourse and the tension of the difficult moment is eased away. But Helen is adamant and turns on Fiona demanding a response to her challenge: 'Well c'mon then Fiona . . . what should we do? (*All laughing.*)'

The tension at this point is heightened and there is yet more laughter to smooth the difficult situation that has developed. Fiona now has little choice but to face the challenge head on and defend her professional credibility. A confrontation has arisen and immediately we notice the change from casual language to serious professional language. Her explanation is couched in the most explicit professional references: 'Well we have to keep the balance . . . they will need different activities for different abilities . . . differentiation . . . and maybe some science . . . and we mustn't ignore the technology curriculum . . .' Fiona defends her professional credibility admirably and the discussion continues. Teachers have to establish and maintain continually their professional credibility amongst their colleagues.

What begins to emerge from this discussion is that the teacher's professional skills extend into areas well beyond the teacher's work in the classroom with children. What we are beginning to see is that the teacher's professional skill may include a very wide range of strategies indeed. Not only does professional skill involve the ability to implement appropriate power relationships to promote the most effective learning with children but also teachers

- have the ability to synthesise a wide range of issues before they can make teaching plans;
- have to be literate in the language of their profession, in order to carry out their work;
- have to have the ability to share and formulate professional knowledge with their fellow professionals;
- have to be prepared to influence and be influenced by the professional beliefs and values of their colleagues; and

- have to have the ability to analyse, define and articulate the immediate context of their work, and the work of their fellow professionals.

For these reasons teachers

- have to be able to establish and maintain continually their professional credibility amongst their colleagues.

Suggestions for teachers

1. With the consent of your colleagues, try recording a staff discussion, student seminar, teaching team meeting or a staff meeting. Select the most interesting five minutes of the recording. Make a note of your reasons for choosing this particular passage.
2. Can you find evidence of teachers analysing, defining or articulating the context in which they work?
3. Can you find any evidence of the discussion being used to share and formulate professional beliefs and values?
4. How will the expression of shared values affect your work or the work of your colleagues?
5. Can you find examples of colleagues establishing their professional credibility? Why did they need to do this? Was their position challenged or was it spontaneous? Why did this happen?
6. Does this recording help you to discover the ways in which you have influenced the work of your colleagues? In what ways have you influenced their work? Try to make a list of the power interests that structure your work. Share these notes with your colleagues. Do they agree with you, or would they suggest something different?

Power in the community: teachers and parents

In the last chapter we saw how teachers negotiate the power relationships amongst themselves and, in turn, how this negotiation
structures the context of a teacher's work. However, teachers are
not the only influence on what can or cannot be achieved in the
classroom with children. Parents also play a very important part in
the education of their children, not only because their values are
transmitted through the children in the classroom but also in the
form of direct contacts with the teacher. Parental contacts with
teachers also affect the learning possibilities and limitations in the
classroom. We can see this happening quite clearly in the following
extract. In this extract the reception class teacher is talking to a
small group of parents whose children are about to enter the reception class.

During the coming term the new intake of eight children would be
arriving in school. An open evening was arranged for the parents of
these children to provide an opportunity to discuss any important
issues. The whole evening was geared to giving parents an informal
opportunity to raise any issues that they felt were important. In the
event, the meeting was well attended with six of the eight children
being represented by at least one parent. The meeting began with a
formal introduction by the head, who then handed over to the reception class teacher, Shirley. Shirley showed the parents around her
classroom where she had laid out some of the most frequently used
equipment. She touched briefly on some of the 'first day' problems
and then invited questions from the parents. Terry was the first parent to speak:

> *Terry:* I wonder if I could . . . I'd like to ask you a question that I find really
> difficult . . . What do you think parents should do in terms of getting a
> youngster ready for school . . . I mean . . . ready to pop off, happy as a lark
> . . . to school on the first day?

Shirley: Er . . . I think they should try to talk a lot about school . . . and maybe they should try and visit the school. They need to go and see the school and the classroom. You could talk to them about what might happen . . . er . . . you could try talking about what they are going to do, like at playtimes and lunch times . . .
Rosemary: (*Vehemently.*) Yes!

The opening question from Terry tells us a great deal about her attitude towards the teacher. The question is hesitant. It begins: 'I wonder if I could . . . I'd like to ask you a question that I find really difficult . . . What do you think parents should do . . .'

Terry has adopted a less dominant identity. She is seeking advice and her hesitant question might imply that she sees the teacher as someone who is superior in status in this conversation. However, besides recognising the professional status of the teacher, we see the conversation slip into more informal terms with: 'What do you think parents should do in terms of getting a youngster ready for school . . . I mean . . . ready to pop off, happy as a lark . . . to school on the first day?'

The language is characterised by short utterances and casual phrases such as 'pop off' and 'happy as a lark'. As the conversation continues it is clear that there are differences of understanding. The teacher, by the very nature of her position, has superior knowledge, but she handles this situation very carefully. She says:

Er . . . I think they should try to talk a lot about school . . . and maybe they should try and visit the school. They need to go and see the school and the classroom. You could talk to them about what might happen . . . er . . . you could try talking about what they are going to do, like at playtimes and lunch times . . .

Here Shirley is hesitant and polite, in her 'You could talk to them . . .' and 'you could try talking about . . .' We can see that she makes suggestions about what the parents might choose to do with their children, rather than telling them what they ought to do. As the conversation continues this difference in status becomes more marked:

Shirley: There's a lot you can do to help your child too. Encourage them to crayon and draw. Make sure you look at books with them. They need to be able to change from shoes into plimsolls on wet days and at PE times . . . On wet days they need to be able to change their wellies . . . and it can be quite difficult, just finding their own Wellingtons . . . so the children need to have their names in everything, so that they can find their own things . . . And lunch boxes . . . a lot of children have a lunch box for the first time . . . and it's quite a problem . . . there's a catch to open. So being able to practise beforehand in the holidays, perhaps on a picnic, is important. You could teach them to open a flask too, so that they can get a drink out . . .

In her professional capacity the teacher begins to use a different kind of language. This contribution is much longer than any of the other contributions. In complete contrast to what has gone before, there are no casual phrases, the utterance is a carefully structured list of things which may help children on their first day at school. In comparison with all the other utterances, it has a much greater degree of formality about it. Nevertheless, it is important to note that there are none of the professional references which were observed in the conversation between teachers in the previous chapter. This teacher is not trying to establish her professional credibility. In this situation it is not necessary in quite the same way as it is when she talks to her colleagues.

In effect, these are new ideas which the teacher is carefully spelling out to the parents. She is continuing to make suggestions rather than tell the parents. She is being helpful and co-operative. Although she is in a position of superior knowledge she encourages the parents to take a full part in the discussion by adopting less dominant power strategies. By encouraging the parents to take part she has a greater opportunity to influence their thinking, to gain a consensus of opinion and ultimately, the consent and co-operation of the parents. It is important for the teacher to work co-operatively with the parents right from the start of the child's education. As a teacher Shirley will be far more effective if she can gain the consent and co-operaton of the parents.

In adopting these procedures, Shirley has a greater chance of communicating her ideas more effectively. We can see this process taking place in the contributions that followed. Paula follows up the teacher's comments with:

Paula: It's interesting 'cos . . . 'Cos what you're saying . . . what you're talking about really is . . . you're not suggesting in any way that erm . . . parents should push the child . . . I mean push the child into thinking about starting school . . . You're saying that what the parent should really be doing is sort of . . . well you could say . . . getting the child in good working order, as it were . . .
Shirley: That's right. Giving them . . .
Terry: You mean . . . Not . . . Not trying to say 'and remember . . . this is school and it's a most important day . . .'. You have to avoid that . . .
Shirley: That's right! (*Laughter.*)
Rosemary: That wouldn't be a good thing to say, would it? I should think it would be quite bad . . .

Shirley: Oh, I think so, 'cos I think that would sort of . . . frighten the child.
Nora: Yes.
Shirley: I think you need to relax the child . . . it's gonna be ordinary . . . it's gonna be just another day, a sort of . . . going out somewhere.

In the first contribution, Paula tries to expand and explore the new ideas that were put forward by the teacher. She says quite simply: 'really what parents have to do is prepare the child for the new demands that school will make upon it.' But if we look at what she actually says, we can see just how much time and effort was needed to grasp the new situation. First of all she attempts to summarise what the teacher has been saying: 'It's interesting 'cos . . . 'Cos what you're saying . . . what you're talking about really is . . . you're not suggesting in any way that erm . . . parents should push the child . . . I mean push the child into thinking about starting school . . .' Then she restates the idea and extends it: 'You're saying that what the parent should really be doing is sort of . . . well you could say . . . getting the child in good working order, as it were . . .' The teacher then confirms with an evaluation that this is exactly what she meant: 'That's right. Giving them . . .' Notice that she also continues the discussion with: 'Giving them . . .'. As we have seen in previous chapters this is a less dominant power strategy for ensuring that the learning continues. However, this is interrupted by Terry who summarises the whole idea again and the teacher again confirms her understanding of what has been said: 'You mean . . . Not . . . Not trying to say 'and remember . . . this is school and it's a most important day . . .'. You have to avoid that . . ./*Shirley:* That's right! (*Laughter.*)'

Terry's interruption was quite a dominant power strategy but the teacher negotiated the power by a variety of less dominant strategies:

- Allowing the parent to speak without interruption.
- Providing a positive evaluation.
- The use of humour which served to release the tension and maintain friendly group relationships.

At this point the teacher was acting in a leadership role, chairing and fostering the development of the discussion. In this way she creates opportunities for the parents to explore the ideas that she has put before them, but she is also laying the foundations for a co-operative relationship between the school and the parents. In this way we can see how new knowledge has to be carefully introduced into the interaction with the parents and opportunities have to be created for parents to make the ideas their own. In this stretch of conversation we can see the teacher helping the parents to 'make the ideas their own' by creating opportunities for them to

- restate the ideas in their own words;
- explore with the group what the ideas might mean and what they imply; and
- explain to each other what they think is intended.

In this way the teacher has introduced new ideas to the parents, but she has not simply told them what is required, she has allowed them to work upon the ideas as a group, so that this particular set of thoughts has now become shared and accepted knowledge in the group. Once knowledge is accepted as shared knowledge within a group, it can be referred to in quite a different way. We see Rosemary refer to the whole idea in her next contribution: 'That wouldn't be a good thing to say, would it? I should think it would be quite bad . . .' She simply refers to the whole idea as it and that is now an accepted part of Rosemary's and the group's thinking. As the discussion continues, we see Shirley work on the group confidence:

> *Shirley:* Oh, I think so, 'cos I think that would sort of . . . frighten the child.
> *Nora:* Yes.
> *Shirley:* I think you need to relax the child . . . it's gonna be ordinary . . . it's gonna be just another day, a sort of . . . going out somewhere.

Here we see Shirley reassure the parents. She tells them that this is just an ordinary event. In this act she creates peer acceptance and good feeling amongst the parents. She succeeds in creating a positive attitude amongst the parents who are naturally concerned about their children's first day of school.

The strategies used by this teacher in this short stretch of conversation were also less dominant strategies, aimed at gaining acceptance, consent and co-operation. They consisted of

- being helpful;
- making suggestions rather than telling the parents what to do;
- being polite;
- allowing time for new ideas to be explored;
- being positive;
- being encouraging; and
- using humour appropriately.

Although it may seem that many of these strategies are common-sense strategies, which might be expected in any adult conversation, it is often the case that parents are not so relaxed and friendly when they visit the teacher and vice versa. Frequently it is a problem which brings parents and teachers together, when all parties feel under greater pressure. It is in circumstances such as these where the professional skills of the teacher to exercise restraint and leadership are put to the test. In the extract included in this chapter this is the key to Shirley's success with the parents. She did not assume a very dominant position and tell the parents what the school expected of them, she talked about the needs of the children and allowed the parents to work out what was required for themselves. She has been a successful leader by assuming less dominant power strategies. She has succeeded by careful negotiation of the power relationships.

Suggestions for teachers

1. With the consent of your colleagues, try carrying out a role play. Work in teams of three. One person will be the teacher, the second person will be an observer/evaluator and the third person will be a parent who is not pleased with the progress of his or her child.
2. Can you find evidence of the teacher negotiating the power relationships? How effective were the power strategies? Could they have been handled differently?
3. Change roles. This time the parent is confused by the National Curriculum and has come into school to find out about it.
4. Can you find evidence of the teacher negotiating the power relationships? How effective were the power strategies? Could they have been handled differently?
5. In your group try making a list of the main sources of concern expressed by parents. What does your group think might be the best ways of handling each of these situations?
6. Share these notes with your colleagues. Do they agree with you, or would they suggest something different?

8

Influences beyond the classroom that affect a teacher's work: power and leadership

In this book so far we have examined the power situation in which a teacher performs his or her professional activities. However, what is not always obvious when teachers are working in their classrooms is that what teachers can or cannot do is influenced by external factors beyond the classroom. In order to explore the work of teachers fully we must also ask ourselves: What are these external influences and how do they affect the work of a teacher?

In the extract which follows two teachers are having a meeting with the headteacher and a local adviser to discuss a school-based in-service course on reading skills in the lower junior school. The names have been changed to preserve anonymity.

After an HMI report that reading standards in the local area were not as high as they might be, Peter, the head, was trying to set up an in-service course for his staff. He was a supportive head and faced the dilemma on the one hand of needing to show that he was doing something about the low reading standards but, on the other hand, not making his staff feel that this course reflected blame for the poor reading standards. He had invited Valerie the local adviser into the school to discuss the problem. Between them they had decided that the best course of action would be for the school to take part in a local reading research project. This would eliminate suggestions that the teachers were being blamed for the poor reading standards, whilst providing the necessary staff development.

Present were Peter, the head, Valerie, the adviser, Ian, the deputy head and Alison, the teacher with responsibility for language. Ian and Alison were going to be jointly responsible for the school's part in the research project. At the point where the extract begins they were discussing the aims of the project and how it might start in the school:

Valerie: I don't think. When I have had headteachers groups, and tried to get us to crystallise the aims of the primary school, for instance, or the aims in reading . . . It is extraordinarily difficult.

Alison: But there isn't just one aim in reading anyhow.

Everyone: (Simultaneously.) Yes. That's right. I know. *(Loud hubbub.)*

Ian: (Over the noise.) This is what I wanted to come out . . .

Alison: (Interrupting.) It's far more complex . . .

Ian: (continuing in spite of Alison's interruption) . . . that there are many different aims, there are many short-term ones . . . more longer-term ones.

Peter: I think maybe . . . an appropriate way . . . I fear that you, . . . that you might be right here, when you say that the teachers think that they are coming on a course . . . and I think my fear is that you will come up against a brick wall at the first meeting, because people will come with certain expectations and you will immediately fling the ball straight back to them and say 'No . . . you're, you're actually going to work it all out.' And they will feel a little bit perplexed if not threatened.

Valerie: Yes. *(Agreeing.)*

Peter: And so . . . maybe, a realistic way to start is to ask them to reflect upon what they actually do now. Now, somewhere . . . in the literature here *(the group had information about the local reading research project)* we have a stated aim of the project, to analyse what we're doing now, against all of the skills that are involved in making an effective reader. *(General 'Yes', and signs of agreement.)* Well you obviously can't expect them to take that kind of lead.

Valerie: No.

Peter: That's not on. But I think you could start by saying to them: what do you do now, in the lower junior school? Now, they can answer that question.

Valerie: Yes.

Peter: Even if they answer nothing.

Valerie: Yes.

Peter: But hopefully the answer is something. Then I think the next question is, Why do you do that? Now I think you're beginning to get a lead . . . into this collection of skills, this analysis of skills, for the business of effective reading. Then I think . . . you could reasonably say to them: 'Now what more could be done then? In the light of what you see, you're aiming at? Your objectives, your goals, whatever, what more could be done? And what would be . . . the most effective way . . . of doing it?' I mean, some of the answers, Valerie, are quite simple. In some cases . . .

Valerie: Yes. *(Agreeing.)*

Peter: You can improve reading standards by giving children time to read books . . .

Valerie: (Interrupts.) It can be, yes. Yes.

Peter: It's as simple as that. Without going into a . . . a very complicated set of erm . . . . analyses.

Valerie: Yes.

Peter: But I think if you can . . . lead them in, in this way . . . without giving them any answers . . . because that would be the course . . . and that's . . . we don't want to do that . . . But I think we are, in duty bound to lead them the right way, because they come full of good will . . . that they are prepared to focus on, maybe for the first time . . . on this particular field . . . that the development of reading in the junior school. And I think all you'll need will be the appropriate carrots at the right time. And the teachers themselves, intuitively in some cases . . .

Valerie: (*Interrupts.*) Yes.

Peter: . . . will begin to clarify their ideas. Then I think we're in business.

Valerie: Yes. Yes.

Ian: (*Interrupts. High pitched voice.*) Erm . . . I think . . . erm . . . Valerie . . . (*hesitant*) I think one . . . point that bears on this . . . and it comes back to a . . . if teachers . . . the business of before and after . . . and the concern that erm . . . immediately this thing starts . . . it is going to have an effect on the way that people think, and the things that they do . . . erm . . . their expectations . . . erm . . . the way in which they . . . approach this whole problem of reading in the . . . er . . . at this particular stage of first juniors, in the junior school. If in fact, one . . . says we need to know what is being done now. And this is . . . as it were . . . ascertained . . . at this first . . . er . . . either at this first session . . . or in . . . as part of the first work . . . er . . . it would seem to me that one could ask . . . questions of the sort that one would be mentioning . . . that require . . . specific responses, that one could . . . if you like . . . at the end of the session . . . you could give exactly the same questions . . .

Valerie: (*Interrupts.*) Yes.

Peter: (*Simultaneously.*) That was my point . . .

Ian: (*continues*) . . . to exactly the same . . . group. And then . . . All right, so you, you, you might notice . . . certain changes, but it does mean that a considerable amount of careful thinking . . . er . . . about, these questions which you are going to ask . . .

Peter: (*Simultaneously.*) Yes. In any case . . .

Ian: . . . in these sessions.

Valerie: (*Interrupts.*) Yes.

Ian: Well immediately the sessions start . . . the, if you want to call it contamination or halo effect . . . or whatever, or . . . i-i-is going to set in . . .

Valerie: (*Very loud high-pitched voice.*) Well I think the interest sets in even before they come. The mere fact that a staff get together and decide . . . shall we go on with this . . . and they come as a team, so that they will always go back, and they will always be . . . discussions in the staffroom about it, I think even from that point . . . you are effecting the school.

Ian: Yes but . . . but I'm still . . . s-saying the point that Peter made, that I . . . sort of combine the idea of asking questions of the sort that Peter suggested . . .

Valerie: Yes.

Ian: with er . . . some of your ideas, would enable one of, for the whole of this teacher group, alone, to have . . . a quite useful . . . before and after description.

Valerie: Yes.

Alison: But then you'd have to keep a . . . or they would have to keep a very careful account of exactly what happened between the before and after . . . so that you could account for . . . the change (*general hubbub*) . . . well I mean what would it prove . . . just that teachers who joined in on reading research groups . . . got better readers at the end . . . or answer questions differently . . .

Ian: W-W-Well, this kind of exercise . . . you don't know what you're gonna prove . . . until you see what you've got.

Peter: Until you've got the last set of questionnaires you don't . . .

Alison: (Interrupts.) Yes. When you get your different answers . . . What, where does it get you?

Ian: Well let me explain to you . . .

Peter: (Interrupts.) Well no, I think you . . . Can I just answer this one . . . it's a fairly specific kinda question . . . erm . . . I'm sorry if we're offending you and we seem to know everything. (*General embarrassed laughs and agreement.*) One is hypothesising here . . . (*Prolonged coughing.*) We could say er . . . during the period of the course . . . the groups have done . . . and the things they will have done will be the things that Valerie has spelled out to us . . . the A,B,C,D and E, I think they were . . . of various kinds. And they have done those things. Now, what you can't be wholly certain . . . that there are changes in emphasis there due to any one of those things you can say that there has been a growth chain, and that these things have happened as well. You'll never get to a point where you can say, by using method A, you get the finite result . . . of method A plus twenty. I don't think you're ever going to get to that stage. I don't think anyone's got that kind of idea in mind . . .

Valerie: Can I, can I suggest something, because of all these good ideas . . . that you're all putting in . . . erm, we were invited to be members of this group . . . and really it's to pick your brains, a lot of it . . . and perhaps to get some work out of you too . . . It would be most helpful if . . . you know nearly everyone in the room has come in with a suggestion . . . that's useful. Would it be asking too much if I asked after you leave here tonight, if you scribble down . . . on a piece of paper, it doesn't matter in what form it is . . . like the things you said Ian, and Alison . . . scribble down whatever you think was the most important contribution you've made to this and send them in to me within the next few days? It would be very helpful, because some very good ideas are coming out of it.

Peter: I like Ian's suggestion, because it er . . . would give your first meeting some structure . . . and er . . . If you just went in and left it completely open ended, you'd have a massive analysis job . . . I liked his idea of these categories. But I think the categories would have to be very carefully thought out . . . And there isn't an awful lot of time to think them out.

At first sight this innocuous and friendly conversation might seem to be very uninteresting and ordinary. But if we examine it closely there is far more happening than might have been expected. The opening contribution by Valerie is particularly interesting: 'I don't think. When I have had headteachers groups, and tried to get us to crystallise the aims of the primary school, for instance, or the aims in reading . . . It is extraordinarily difficult.' The language she is using here makes many assumptions. For example anyone taking part in this conversation would need to know what she meant by the aims of the primary school and the aims in reading. Although she explains that these are extraordinarily difficult to formulate, the fact that she is talking about them implies that she expects the other participants in the conversation to know at least something about them. The inference here is that anyone wishing to take part in this kind of conversation must be able to use the professional language forms which refer to it and that teachers must be conversant with the wider professional issues which inform their work: teachers need to be able to use the professional language associated with their work.

It was perhaps this need to demonstrate and establish this particular professional competence which prompted Alison to make a comment that did not have any direct bearing on the previous comment. Valerie had not attempted to suggest that there was only one aim to reading, but Alison countered with: 'But there isn't just one aim in reading anyhow.' Alison's comment, although it was not entirely relevant was clearly important, because it prompted a further exchange from the other teacher present:

> Everyone: (Simultaneously.) Yes. That's right. I know. (Loud hubbub.)
> Ian: (Over the noise.) This is what I wanted to come out . . .
> Alison: (Interrupting.) It's far more complex . . .
> Ian: (Continuing in spite of Alison's interruption) . . . that there are many different aims, there are many short-term ones . . . more longer-term ones.

Here we see Ian agreeing with Alison, supporting her point and apparently extending it. Although the content of what he says adds little to what has already been said, he has demonstrated that he too knows about the aims of reading. In this way the teachers, who are the lower-status members of this particular group, have established their credentials and their right to take part in this conversation as bona fide participants.

Interestingly, once this is done, Peter steps in quickly and says: 'I think maybe . . . an appropriate way . . . I fear that you, . . . that you might be right here, when you say that the teachers think that they are coming on a course . . .' He seems to be hesitant and changes what he is going to say twice before he finally says what he intends. The hesitations are important because they create space between the earlier part of the interaction and what is to follow. A break of this kind can be a clear indicator to the participants that he is about to change the course of the conversation. The words he uses suggest that he is going to change the conversation from arguing about the aims of reading to suggesting a way ahead for developing the course.

We may interpret this move in several ways. First of all we might think that this was the action of a good pragmatic head, who was trying to keep the discussion moving in a positive direction and he certainly was. However, Peter was under pressure to be seen to be doing something about the low reading standards in the area; therefore, we might interpret this as a dominant power strategy. He has deliberately created a break, then re-framed the discussion in order to address his own pressures. This is quite obvious later in the discussion when he steers the group towards looking at the state of reading in the school at the present time and then, almost too quickly, follows it up with: 'Then I think . . . you could reasonably say to them: "Now what more could be done then? In the light of what you see, you're aiming at? Your objectives, your goals, whatever, what more could be done? And what would be . . . the most effective way . . . of doing it.?" ' His insistence on 'what more could be done?' expresses his real concerns in the matter. Equally, just as the teachers in previous extracts reinforced their positions by repetition, we can see that Peter also repeats this point. He is insisting that this is a focal point of the discussion. In effect he structures the possibilities for future action by changing the direction of the discussion.

In Peter's next substantial contribution to the discussion we learn a great deal about how he operates with his staff. First he talks about leading his staff, suggesting that there is a particular direction in which he wants them to go, but then he insists that it would be wrong to give them the answers. Here Peter is describing the constructively ambiguous identity which he adopts to achieve as much as he can with his staff. Just as the teachers in the previous chapters led their pupils by being different people with different individuals, so Peter leads his staff by being constructively ambiguous. He knows that any change in attitudes amongst his staff will have to be brought about by the consent of the staff themselves, they must discover their own answers. On the other hand, he is talking about structuring the situation to ensure that the answers which his staff discover are not contrary to the general direction in which he sees the school moving. Peter structures the situation for his staff and adopts a constructively ambiguous identity to enable him to get his work done.

Taking a general view of Peter's operation with his staff, we can see that in arranging the meeting he was responding to his own pressures from the HMI report. As a head he had to do something about the reportedly low reading standards. In opting to join a research project rather than have a direct in-service course, he can be more certain of gaining the consent and co-operation of his staff. These two actions have satisfied the needs of two of the groups of people who have interests in his work and with whom he works.

The outcome of this action is that he has structured the ways in which his staff will act. In effect he has structured the context in which his staff will work. Within this context he operates with a constructively ambiguous identity to enable him to get his work done. This is important, because it highlights the point that teachers themselves work in a carefully structured power situation. What teachers can achieve in their classrooms is not merely constrained by the teaching concerns of the classroom teacher but also what teachers do in their classrooms is structured by external pressures.

Another interesting feature of this conversation was the part played by Valerie, the adviser. Valerie intersperses 'yes' into the conversation no less than ten times in this short extract. Why does she do this? Is it just an annoying habit, or does she do it with a purpose in mind? Linguistically we might think that she is providing feedback in the conversation to show the speaker that she has understood the message, but if this is the case why didn't Ian and Alison also demonstrate this behaviour? Bearing in mind the fact that Peter had called Valerie in to help him solve a problem, there is possibly another explanation. In terms of the power strategies we can gain some clues by looking at the structure of the discourse. We can see how Valerie supports Peter in this exchange:

SITUATION
Peter: But hopefully the answer is something.
PROBLEM
Then I think the next question is, Why do you do that? Now I think you're beginning to get a lead . . . into this collection of skills, this analysis of skills, for the business of effective reading. Then I think . . . you could reasonably say to them: 'Now what more could be done then? In the light of what you see, you're aiming at? Your objectives, your goals, whatever, what more could be done? And what would be . . . the most effective way . . . of doing it?'
SOLUTION
I mean, some of the answers, Valerie, are quite simple. In some cases . . .
EVALUATION
Valerie: Yes. (*Agreeing.*)

By agreeing here Valerie provides an evaluation which completes the discourse structure. This strategy makes it more difficult for the other participants to comment upon the discourse or change its direction. But the matter does not end here. Peter chooses to reinforce his position with two further repetitions, which Valerie again vigorously supports:

REPEAT SOLUTION
Peter: You can improve reading standards by giving children time to read books . . .

REPEAT EVALUATION
Valerie: (Interrupts.) It can be, yes. Yes.

Notice here how Valerie uses repetition to affirm and reaffirm her supporting position. Then finally:

REPEAT SOLUTION
Peter: It's as simple as that. Without going into a . . . a very complicated set of erm . . . analyses.
REPEAT EVALUATION
Valerie: Yes.

We see the same in the next contribution as Peter continues:

But I think if you can . . . lead them in, in this way . . . without giving them any answers . . . because that would be the course . . . and that's . . . we don't want to do that . . . But I think we are, in duty bound to lead them the right way, because they come full of good will . . . that they are prepared to focus on, maybe for the first time . . . on this particular field . . . that the development of reading in the junior school. And I think all you'll need will be the appropriate carrots at the right time. And the teachers themselves, intuitively in some cases . . .
Valerie: (Interrupts.) Yes.

Peter puts a situation, problem and solution, whilst Valerie provides the evaluation, effectively inhibiting any other contributions. In this way Valerie helps Peter to structure the possibilities of the future discussion. Working together they are a powerful team. Between them they can set up very dominant power strategies.

A further example of the power relationships in the discourse occurred towards the end of the meeting when Alison, who had seemed unconvinced throughout the meeting, quite legitimately challenged the whole purpose of the reading research project: '. . . Well I mean what would it prove . . . just that teachers who joined in on reading research groups . . . got better readers at the end . . . or answer questions differently . . .'

She asks 'what would it prove?' This is an overt challenge which could easily have resulted in confrontation and could easily have destroyed all of the effort that had gone into structuring the meeting so far. So how did each of the participants respond? Ian adopted a less dominant power strategy and questioned Alison's assumption that one could or should specify in advance what could be proved: 'W-W-Well, this kind of exercise . . . you don't know what you're gonna prove . . . until you see what you've got.' In this comment he indicates his support for the rest of the meeting and lack of support for the direction in which Alison is taking the discussion. Peter reaffirms Ian's comment with: 'Until you've got the last set of questionnaires you don't . . .' But Alison is adamant. She clearly finds the answers unacceptable. Not only does she interrupt Peter before he has finished but she also uses repetition to bring the discourse back to its former position of possible confrontation: '(*Interrupts.*) Yes. When you get your different answers . . . What, where does it get you?'

How do the other participants respond to this further challenge? Ian adopts a more dominant power strategy in his attempt to 'explain' to Alison. But Peter clearly felt that this was not the answer to the problem. He could not leave this situation to chance and he stepped in with a combination of less dominant strategies. First he adopts a less dominant strategy in recognising the legitimacy of the point Alison is making and implies that she deserves a fair hearing: (*Interrupts.*) Well no, I think you . . . Can I just answer this one . . . it's a fairly specific kinda question . . . erm . . .' Then he totally defuses the situation, in effect restoring friendly relationships with an act of politeness: 'I'm sorry if we're offending you and we seem to know everything. (*General embarrassed laughs and agreement.*)' Then he begins to renegotiate the power relationships in the discussion by reframing it:

> One is hypothesising here . . . (*Prolonged coughing.*) We could say er . . . during the period of the course . . . the groups have done . . . and the things they will have done will be the things that Valerie has spelled out to us . . . the A,B,C,D and E, I think they were . . . of various kinds. And they have done those things. Now, what you can't be wholly certain . . . that there are changes in emphasis due to any one of those things you can say that there has been a growth chain and that these things have happened as well. You'll never get to a point where you can say, by using method A, you get the finite result . . . of method A plus twenty. I don't think you're ever going to get to that stage. I don't think anyone's got that kind of idea in mind . . .

In this lengthy contribution he presents a situation, problem, solution and an evaluation. This, as we have seen in previous examples, is a dominant power strategy which inhibits comment from the other participants. He effectively tells Alison that her point has been dealt with and that is the end of the matter. What is particularly interesting is the contribution made by Valerie immediately following Peter's statement: 'Can I, can I suggest something, because of all these good ideas . . . that you're all putting in . . .'As soon as Peter has finished, Valerie steps in and begins to bring the meeting to a close. This is a powerfully supportive move for two reasons: first it moves the discourse on and ensures that Alison will not make a further challenge. Secondly, bringing the meeting to a close at this point is a safety measure. It implies that the discussion is over and all that remains to be done is the 'tidying up'. This further precludes the possibility of Alison re-opening the discussion.

Valerie's concluding contribution is particularly interesting and deserves detailed discussion. To begin with she adopts a less dominant power strategy by 'making a suggestion'. She seems to imply that the participants need not accept what she has to say: 'Can I, can I suggest something.' She continues by being complimentary about the 'good ideas' which everyone has contributed: 'because of all these good ideas . . . that you're all putting in . . . erm.'

This of course was a debatable point, especially in the case of Alison, who challenged the discussion in every contribution she made. Then Valerie reminds the participants of their special group relationship: 'we were invited to be members of this group . . . and really it's to pick your brains, a lot of it . . . and perhaps to get some work out of you too . . .' Here she is drawing on peer group pressure. This is a powerful social control strategy, because it constrains members of the group to behave in a manner cognisant with the values of the group. She then follows this with a suggestion that this group was chosen so that its 'brains could be picked' yet, in reality, the head, deputy and language co-ordinator were the group that might have been expected to carry out this kind of exercise. Therefore this was another compliment suggesting that the participants had something very special to contribute. Valerie is really working hard to establish group coherence at this point. Then she appeals to the better nature of the participants by asking a 'favour':

> It would be most helpful if . . . you know nearly everyone in the room has come in with a suggestion . . . that's useful. Would it be asking too much if I asked after you leave here tonight, if you scribble down . . . on a piece of paper, it doesn't matter in what form it is . . . like the things you said Ian, and Alison . . . scribble down whatever you think was the most important contribution you've made to this and send them in to me within the next few days?

Then she ends with a further compliment to the group: 'It would be very helpful, because some very good ideas are coming out of it.' From all of the examples we have examined so far it now becomes apparent that politeness is an important and powerful leadership strategy.

Apart from being a polite friendly person, what reason could Valerie have had for adopting this wide range of strategies? Seen from the point of the power situation this was a masterstroke. Valerie adopted a less dominant power strategy which was more likely to secure consent and co-operation, then she established warm personal relationships with compliments, then she worked on the group coherence. Anyone challenging or disagreeing with her at the point when she asked a 'favour' would have appeared to be extremely rude and ill-mannered. But why was that 'favour' so important?

The 'favour' was 'to scribble down the most important contribution you have made and send it to me in the next few days'. Asking participants to focus on their most important contribution requires them to think positively. Thinking positively is more likely to result in co-operation and consent and less likely to result in challenge. The request to send the results to Valerie has several effects. First of all, it ensures that in the midst of all their other professional concerns, the participants will not simply go away and forget about it. It structures the situation in such a way that the participants are encouraged to commit themselves to becoming actively involved in the reading research project.

Finally, the notes will presumably provide Valerie with a great deal of information about the state of play with different individuals. This will help her to discover where there are likely to be possibilities for future action and where support may be necessary. This information will help her to structure future situations in the most useful and positive ways. In effect, Valerie has very neatly structured the future direction of the reading project. She has been a good leader and executed her responsibilities most effectively.

We can see this point emphasised in the final contribution made by Peter, who also takes the opportunity to structure the future development of the reading project. Peter encourages the teachers at the meeting to develop their thinking and actions in an appropriate manner; thus in a very positive way he too structures the future action of the teachers. But what can a conversation of this kind tell us about the work of teachers?

What can we learn about the work of teachers?

First, this extract is important because it illustrates further power strategies. Here we can see some very positive and effective strategies in use. For example we see the following:

- Creating a break in the discourse then changing the direction of the discussion, as Peter did, right at the beginning.
- Two people working together manipulating the structure of the discourse are a very powerful influence.
- Dominant power relationships can be set up by overt explanations.

Situations can be positively structured by adopting the following less dominant power relationships:

- Recognising the legitimacy of another person's point.
- Acts of politeness.
- Making 'suggestions'.
- Praising and being complimentary.
- Drawing on peer group pressure.
- Establishing group coherence.
- Asking 'favours'.
- Appealing to the better natures of the other participants.
- Being encouraging.
- Encouraging positive thinking.
- Encouraging further activity from the participants.
- Encouraging further commitment.

Many teachers will recognise these strategies as some of the most helpful and powerful alternatives open to them in the classroom with children. However, besides providing further insights into how teachers operate in the classroom, this extract also provides clues about other aspects of a teacher's work.

In this extract we have seen two very good leaders at work. Their work involves structuring the context in which the teachers will work. As Peter put it, 'leading but not giving the answers'. Observing how the interaction is structured for teachers helps us to understand that teachers work within a very clearly defined power situation. Part of the power situation is generated within the classroom and school, but much of it is not.

Many of the constraints which determine what teachers will do are generated from external pressures. Thus we can begin to understand that what a teacher does is not only determined by the learning needs of the children but also by external demands. These are the external demands put upon schools by society. In effect, we might say that teachers work at the interface between the learning needs of children and the demands put upon the education system by society.

These two major demands upon teachers structure the power context in which teachers work, and from the discussion we have seen that just as teachers structure the possibilities of future action for their pupils, so the work of teachers is also structured. Further, it is important that teachers recognise the power context in which they work.

This extract provides us with some important insights into the nature of leadership as it is operated by teachers and upon teachers. In a very general way we can begin to see that leadership is a delicate balance between consent and domination. What this extract seems to show is that the most successful power strategies are those which might be described as not open to challenge.

But this does not necessarily imply those strategies which dominate and attempt to hold the floor are the most effective. For instance, Alison's dominant strategy did not succeed in influencing the discussion because the other participants did not lend their consent. When Alison challenged the arguments that had been put forward, her efforts were quickly dealt with using a variety of strategies. Powerful acts of leadership such as those observed in Valerie's concluding comments are acts which work at gaining the consent of the participants. Therefore we might say that the most effective power strategies are those which attract the greater degree of consent over the longest periods of time.

In terms of power strategies, it may well be the case that the least dominant power strategies result in the most effective, least contestable acts of leadership, because they secure the greater consent. Therefore, acts of leadership, far from dominating the participants present, may well be far more concerned with firm but gentle influence. Acts of leadership aim at constructing situations which will gain consent over the longest periods of time.

As we have seen in this extract, constructing situations which secure consent requires skilful manipulation of the power situation. From the contributions made by Valerie and Peter we have seen that some of the skills of leadership involved the following:

- Assessing the most effective power strategies in a specific power situation.
- Using less dominant power strategies such as politeness to encourage consent and co-operation.
- Being sensitive to the power relationships and using them effectively, by being complimentary and reinforcing the cohesion of the group.
- Being able to address the needs and motivations of the other participants, by structuring the situation in such a way that the school was seen to be taking part in a research project, rather than sending the staff on an in-service course because the reading standards in the school were low.
- Being able to influence the purpose of a discussion by re-framing it and changing the subject where necessary.
- Being able to manipulate the structure of the discourse to circumscribe the future actions of others.

Generally, leadership involves the ability to recognise the power relationships in a particular group of people, the ability to operate effectively within those constraints and the ability to renegotiate the power relationships which will structure future actions. In this context, acts of leadership might truly be described as structuring the field of action for others – circumscribing the possibilities of future actions (Foucault, 1982).

Suggestions for teachers

1. With the consent of your colleagues, try recording a staff discussion, student seminar, teaching team meeting, a staff meeting or a general parents' meeting. Select the most interesting five minutes of the recording. Make a note of your reasons for choosing this particular passage.
2. Can you find evidence of power strategies during the meeting? By whom were they performed? What effect did they have upon the meeting? How did the other participants respond? How effective were the power strategies?
3. What reasons do you think the participants had in this meeting for carrying out their power strategies?
4. How do you think these power strategies will affect your work? How will they affect the work of your colleagues?
5. If you have carried out this activity with a group of teachers, share your findings with them. Did they pick out the same power strategies? Were there reasons why you picked out the same or different power strategies? Why was this?
6. Did all the group interpret the meeting in the same way? What were the similarities and differences? If there were differences how could you explain them?
7. Does this recording help you to discover the external influences which structure your particular teaching situation? Make a list of the external power influences which structure your work. Share these notes with your colleagues. Do the same external influences structure their work or are they different?

9

The influences on teachers' work beyond the school: the wider power context

The influences which determine what a teacher does are not only to be found in the classroom and the school but also in the wider community. The recent introduction of standard attainment tasks (SATs) for seven-year-olds illustrates some of the influences of the wider community on what teachers do in their classrooms.

Prior to April 1991 the Conservative government, concerned that educational standards were falling, introduced a national assessment system of SATs for seven-year-old children. The complexity of the tests during the research and trial period gave rise to adverse comments and concern amongst parents and teachers. It was therefore not surprising that by the time the SATs were first used in schools during March and May 1991, the 'SATs debate' had reached the headlines of the national newspapers.

At this point it is important to point out that the articles illustrating the SATs' issue, unlike the extracts in the previous chapters, are pre-packaged interpretations of events rather than the events themselves. The inferences that can be drawn from interpretive material of this kind are far more speculative and tentative than the inferences of earlier chapters. Nevertheless, the news reports of the period present us with an interesting and instructive case study.

In the *Guardian* on 2 April 1991 an article entitled 'When the talking has to stop' appeared expressing teachers' concerns about the following:

- The amount of paper teachers had to read prior to testing.
- The complicated instructions.
- How relationships with the children suffered during testing.
- How the younger children had to be kept occupied for long periods whilst the teacher was busy testing the older children.
- How much learning time was lost to testing.

- That the test results did not tell the teacher anything that he or she did not already know.
- A great deal of money was spent on testing which would have been better spent elsewhere.
- The tests were patronising for the brighter children.
- Teachers were worried about the hours spent recording results and conducting individual interviews.
- All the other children 'earwigged' and knew the answers to the questions before it was their turn to be tested.

On the other hand the teachers represented in this article:

- accept that testing is necessary;
- accept that testing is here to stay; and
- didn't think that the children being tested felt any real pressure.

The teachers were naturally concerned about the educational effects upon the children's learning and the amount of time taken up by testing and recording. Whilst teachers might normally consider testing to be part of the educational process, in this particular form the testing was so complicated that it inhibited the educational process. In its proposed form testing prevented teachers from pursuing their professional activity, that of educating children.

Also in the *Guardian* on 2nd April an article entitled 'Mums and dad's in the dark' expressed the following parental concerns:

- The tests will disrupt children's learning.
- They will waste children's time.
- The tests will be stressful for children.
- Parents have not been told enough about the tests.
- Parents wanted personal reports on the progress of their children, but they did not want the reports to be made public.
- Seven is too young for testing and labelling children as possible failures.
- If the reports are made public more time will be spent on 'pulling up' the poorer children and not stretching the brighter children.
- The tests would make a lot of work for teachers.

Whilst the parents were naturally expressing concerns for their own particular children, their complaints were very similar to those of the teachers. Their concerns centred on the emotional and educational well-being of the children. As far as the SATs debate was concerned the parents' and teachers' views were in close alignment, critical of SATs.

However, we might also describe these reasons as professional. They are reasons which prevent parents from carrying on their role of parenting, that of bringing up happy, well-balanced children. Interestingly, not everyone supported these views. In the same paper at the same time there also appeared an article entitled: 'A testing time for seven-year-olds' written by the director of the National Foundation for Educational Research which drew up the tests. This article takes each of the criticisms of the tests in turn and puts them in a completely different light, making the following points:

- SATs may brand children of seven as failures, but we need to know this so that they can be helped to catch up.
- If teachers teach to the test this is not necessarily a bad thing, because it will raise educational standards and provide a balanced curriculum.
- The suggestion that SATs are unmanageable and must be scrapped is untrue. They have simply been reduced to interesting and enjoyable activities for children.
- The criticism that SATs did not tell teachers anything they did not already know is not true. Research showed that there was a difference.
- The claim that it would be sufficient to rely on teacher assessments and SATs were not needed would not meet the needs of a standardised national assessment system.

Here is an article expressing outright support for the testing system. It challenges the views of teachers and parents. But if we look carefully at the reasons given, they are also very professional reasons. They address the criticisms of testing and point out that they are not really criticisms but, in the main, advantages. Again we might describe these reasons as professional reasons put forward by a researcher for the purpose of allowing the researcher to continue with the professional activity of researching without disruption.

Meanwhile at a more local level, on 11 April in the *Express and Echo* in Exeter, Devon, several local dignitaries were taking the opportunity to make their contribution to the debate. A university professor stated:

- The tests will not be traumatic for children.
- They are not like the eleven-plus examination, more like normal classroom activities.
- Parents have no cause for concern about the tests.
- The tests had been simplified since the trial run the previous year.

A principal officer of the National Union of Teachers in the South West Region stated:

- There should not be any testing for seven-year-olds.

- The ordinary diagnostic processes of teaching are adequate to assess children's progress.
- The tests have worried parents who are buying up stocks of suggested texts.
- The tests are taking far longer than the time allowed for them.

And a South West Education Committee Chairman stated:

- Assessment should be welcomed but the present system may well need to be modified.
- SATs are an improvement to the education system.
- There is a possibility that teachers may spend too much time testing and the government may need to review this.
- He was confident that the tests in reality would be far less alarming than the teaching unions had suggested.

Again by looking at the arguments in this article very carefully we can see that they too are equally made for professional reasons.

By 24 April others were beginning to enter the debate. In *The Times Educational Supplement* an adviser on assessment wrote an article entitled 'Admissible evidence', questioning the nature of achievement and underlying value of testing seven-year-olds. It made the following points:

- It is difficult to know exactly what should count as evidence of achievement and what should not.
- Achievement should not be divorced from the context in which the achievement is reached.

What we begin to see from these articles is that when a contentious educational issue arises it is likely to be responded to by various groups, who are not teachers, but who have a have a direct interest in what teachers do in their classrooms. The groups that emerged in this debate were parents, teachers, researchers and academics, teaching unions, professional bodies, such as the advisory service, and civil servants. These are the groups who have a power interest in a teacher's work. In a different debate other interest groups may have arisen such as the churches, the judicial system, social workers, the medical service, etc.

However, if we look closely at the arguments put forward about SATs it is clear that they were put forward for professional reasons, that is, they were put forward because they were reasons which were preventing a particular interest group from pursuing its own particular professional activities. They were a protest against change. In this sense it is a mistake to think of the groups as simply interest groups because the groups were actually in competition with each other, protecting their own rights to continue practising their professional activities without disruption. What we are seeing here is not simply interest groups but power groups 'competing against each other to make their voices heard' (Sola and Bennett, 1985). Therefore, in any discussion of what teachers are and what they do, we must begin by thinking about teachers as:

- a power group amongst other power groups in society;
- involved in competing power groups in society, protecting their rights to continue their professional activities without disruption; and
- operating in a system of power relationships in the wider society.

Seen from this point of view the articles in the press are particularly revealing. They can help us to understand a great deal about the nature of the power groups, the power context of the wider society and how it affects teachers.

Teachers and the power context of the wider society

During the period of March and April 1991 preparations were being made for the first attempt at testing all seven-year-olds in England and Wales. However, the testing of children in Scotland had been piloted earlier and had caused considerable concern amongst teachers and parents. Large numbers of parents in Scotland withdrew their children from school, refusing to allow them to be tested. Parents in England and Wales, alerted by events in Scotland, also challenged the policies of the Conservative government by threatening to keep their children at home during the testing period.

Although in Scotland this had proved to be a loop-hole in the law and was a powerful challenge to the government, the same was not true in England and Wales where the law was slightly different. In a dominant power strategy parents in England and Wales were reminded that under the 1944 Education Act, parents were legally required to send their children to school. Parents whose children failed to attend school would face prosecution and possible imprisonment if convicted. Here we see how the government was circumscribing the possibilities for the future actions of parents. It was assuming a dominant identity and using dominant power strategies, drawing upon the power invested in it by the state to enforce its own legislation. This caused many parents to become more entrenched in their position and it heightened the confrontation.

In the meantime at their Easter conference, the National Union of Teachers was debating a move to boycott testing in schools. However, many teachers felt that this move towards confrontation would leave the government little room for manoeuvre. There would be no alternative for the government but to take firm action, which could result in an even more difficult situation for teachers. Finally, at their conference NUT members voted heavily against boycotting testing. A compromise was reached and *The Independent* on 2 May reported that 'Instead of the boycott, the union will campaign to persuade parents and school governors that the tests are damaging to children's education.' In many ways this was a surprising statement to make. After all, the teachers' grievance was with the government not with the parents and governors, who had already been vociferous in expressing their concern about the tests. Parents and governors were the last people who needed to be persuaded about the teachers' position. So why was this statement made?

In terms of the power context we might describe this as a 'shot across the bows' of the Conservative government. Remembering that the most effective power strategies are those which secure consent, challenges to leadership can usually be contained as long as they are challenges made by only one power group. However, Chapter 8 (the extracts of Peter the headteacher and Valerie the adviser) illustrates the point that when two power groups work together they are extremely powerful. Challenges made by combined power groups are far more difficult to contain. In this sense, the statement by the teachers' union was crucial to structuring the possibilities for what might happen in the future. We might interpret it as a statement to the government of the teachers' intention to combine with parents and governors in challenging SATs. This powerful combination would cause a loud outcry which would be damaging to the leadership credibility of the government.

The warning was sufficient. In an election year, when the Conservative government was anxious to limit the outcry against SATs and the damage to its credibility, the situation changed dramatically. During the same week the position in Scotland suddenly improved after 'surprisingly amicable talks with the education authority' ('Teachers throw out boycott on testing' in *The Independent*, 2 May 1991). In England and Wales education authorities began to take a hard line with schools threatening to suspend SATs testing. Headteachers began advising parents that it was illegal to keep their children away from school. In schools where testing had been suspended, it was resumed despite protests from parents. But what happened to bring this about? How can we explain this in terms of the wider power context? Mr Kenneth Clarke, the Secretary of State for Education, was reported to have said: 'We will look closely at the experience of administering the tests this year to see whether they need to be made simpler to administer, or improved in other ways.' (ibid.) This apparent climb down on the part of the government resulted in an immediate improvement in the situation, but it was only a temporary measure. Although the first round of the power struggle went to the teachers and parents, their position was still extremely tentative. An editorial appeared in *The Times Educational Supplement* on 10 May summing up the situation, suggesting that although teachers and parents may cause the government to reconsider its position, such a move may force ministers to think more seriously about SATs:

> These laudable aims have made SATs time consuming and complicated. But the more teachers complain that they are impossible, the more Kenneth Clarke – who last week announced that he was willing to scale down the whole model still further – will be tempted to throw the whole lot out of the window and go for the simple 'pencil and paper' tests Mrs Thatcher wanted in the first place
> (*The Times Educational Supplement*, 10 May 1991).

In *The Times Educational Supplement* on 17 May in an article entitled 'We'll accept changes', Eggar stated:

- Government ministers have accepted that current tests for seven-year-olds in schools have to be made more manageable.
- Ministers are also concerned that the tests for fourteen-year-olds may also be time consuming and overelaborate.
- Ministers will not opt for a wholesale switch, so far, to formal exams.

Here was the first real indication that the Conservative government was prepared to compromise, but not very far. It was a small but transient victory for the teachers and parents. The confrontation had been temporarily averted, but it had not gone away completely. Hidden amongst the promises to reconsider was the threat that ministers might yet return to the Thatcher ideal of pencil and paper tests for seven-year-olds. These were cheaper to administer and would readily yield the information about teaching standards which the government wanted and which they claimed parents wanted.

From these events we might infer the following:

- The power context in the wider society is an activity of compromise.

- The power context in the wider society is such that attempting to solve one dilemma frequently raises further more serious dilemmas.

The SATs debate illustrates how the wider power context affects teachers in two ways: first as a professional group; and secondly in the day-to-day work of individual teachers in their classrooms.

The effects of the SATs debate on teachers as a professional group

The fact that SATs provoked so much concern from teachers as a group in the first place is very interesting. In different circumstances it might be expected that teachers would have considered assessment and the monitoring of pupil progress to be one of their most important professional activities. So why were teachers so concerned about it? The concern expressed could not have been about assessment itself, since most teachers would have considered this to be an important part of their work.

A possible explanation for this concern may lie in the way in which SATs were introduced. The series of events leading up to the introduction of SATs might be described as follows. As far back as Callaghan's Ruskin College speech there had been national concern about standards in education. From the leadership point of view, it was important that the government were seen to be doing something to improve standards in education. The government set up three research consortia to devise tests which would produce a national system of assessment. The tests were trialled and evaluated by research foundations and academic institutions, then presented to teachers for introduction into schools.

Seen in this way the SATs debate seems innocuous, but the difficulty was that very few teachers were consulted or involved in the SATs trials. The tests themselves were kept secret until they had been trialled in schools and at the point of introducing them into schools generally only a small proportion of the teaching force knew anything about them. Because the tests were devised by the educational establishment, rather than teachers, they were far too complicated to operate in most primary school classrooms.

This situation, not surprisingly, was challenged by parents and teachers. If parents and teachers had been consulted, or at least informed, at an earlier stage in the development of the SATs, the tests might have been simpler and their introduction would probably have provoked less anger. In short, the SATs debate illustrates the point that it may not be the policy itself that provoked a negative response, but the way in which it was presented in terms of power strategies.

The SATs debate highlights the point that

- the management of effective power relationships is a two-way process; and
- leadership requires the consent of those who are led and is not merely a process of domination.

In the SATs debate the government were not without blame for their poor leadership strategies, but the teachers themselves were also not without blame. In reality, before this debate the power of teachers had already been considerably reduced by political means. However, as the debate began to unfold, teachers became even more powerless. In order to have any effect in this particular power context, teachers needed to be able to propose their own system of national testing early in the debate. Teachers are after all professional educators whose main concern should have been the monitoring and assessing of pupil progress both individually and nationally.

If teachers had been in a position to address this professional issue at an earlier stage with convincing arguments, they would have entered the assessment debate in a far more powerful position. As it was, teachers offered no convincing argument in the assessment debate. They did not successfully defend their professional expertise and therefore left their professional credibility open to challenge.

Perhaps the most important lesson to be learnt from the SATs debate for teachers as a professional group is that teachers need to establish and defend their professional credibility amongst other power groups in the wider power context.

The effects of the SATs debate on teachers as individuals

The effect of SATs upon individual teachers in their classrooms has been enormous. Although most teachers would not have been averse to a national system of testing, they are now faced with a system of testing with a very heavy administrative workload and tests which are almost impossible to operate in the classroom even with auxiliary help. Teachers have been left to perform tests which they claim do not tell them anything they did not already know about their pupils.

However, and perhaps more seriously, accepting the stalemate attendant on the general election results, created problems for teachers and their relationships with parents. During the SATs debate teachers had formed a close and powerful alliance with parents. Accepting the hiatus in the situation meant that teachers who had threatened to boycott the tests now had to do an 'about turn' and administer the tests in spite of protests from parents. An article appeared in *The Times Educational Supplement* on 17 May 1991 indicating that teachers who had acquiesced and administered the SATs had left themselves in an awkward situation with parents who were still anxious about the effects upon their children:

> Where passions may be running high, how can you [teachers] maintain your professional integrity without compromising the good working relationship you have with parents who have chosen to withdraw their children from testing? . . . Those parents who have spoken to teachers will have met with a mix of honesty and professional pragmatism.

Schools and teachers have been left in a very difficult situation of flying in the face of parental protests, which has seriously damaged the parent/teacher partnership in education. The degree to which the relationship between parents and teachers has been professionally compromised was expressed in 'Professional pragmatism' in *The Times Educational Supplement*, 17 May 1991:

> Those parents who have spoken to teachers will have met with a mix of honesty and professional pragmatism. Explains one year 2 teacher: 'Parents have come to me, wanting to know what SATs mean and whether I think they're useful. I've been saying to them that they're a waste of time and that I don't think they'll give any new information to parents or to teachers.' He also tells them that the activities are harmless. 'At worst, it's boring,' he smiles.

Relationships between teachers and their classes have also been damaged. As one teacher put it:

> My class learned a lot. They learned that, however excited they were about their achievements, however anxious about their misunderstandings, I was not interested 'just now' and that meant almost all day. They learned that if they were six years old instead of seven years – year 1 instead of year 2 – then they really hadn't a chance of my time. . . My year two's, my strugglers, began to realise that they were being sorted and graded however hard I tried to be positive. They looked more and more anxious as they scanned my scribbles and notes . . . Meanwhile, some year 1 children, in their innocence, asked if they could join in only to suffer repeated rejection ('The high price of independence' in *The Times Educational Supplement* 24 May 1991).

And in the *Guardian* on 2 April 1991 (in an article by David Ward):

> Janet Gilvray remembers how basic relationships with pupils had to be rebuilt last year. 'When the local authority told us we could stop the pilots, I stopped my class right in the middle of a test. We did nothing for

the rest of the day except talk to each other. The children had so much to tell me: I had not been able to listen to them for five weeks.' The problem was that while she was assessing a group of children against a chosen attainment target, the rest had to be kept at bay.

'Mopping up in a morning' in *The Times Educational Supplement*, 24 May 1991, illustrates some of the practical difficulties teachers face:

Monday, pm: Sitting surrounded by SAT materials and my own copious notes. I try to sort out SAT science 1, floating and sinking, eventually deciding that once I've got started with the children all will become clear.

Tuesday, 8am: Arrive at school nice and early (the head is out, I am the deputy but have foreseen no difficulties with the day). The other year teacher is just leaving and I wonder if she is giving up already. She tells me the school has been broken into.

The office has been wrecked and there are little piles of copper and silver coins lying in the playground: luckily no larger amounts have been left in the school. . .

The day continues in this vein and eventually the teacher concluded:

A banana which floats at 9.30 sinks at 3 pm.

A bathroom towel is useful, but not if it is put in the water.

A bathroom towel does not float. This teacher is 'doing her best' but reality keeps getting in the way.

Perhaps the most important lessons to be learnt for individual teachers in their classrooms are as follows:

- National issues in the wider power context affect what teachers can and cannot do in their classrooms.
- National issues such as the general election, which may not be of direct educational concern, have a direct effect upon what teachers may or may not do in their classrooms.
- Teachers need to be active in the wider power context if they wish to protect their professional credibility and defend their right to continue in professional practice.

Suggestions for teachers

1. Imagine that you were the Secretary of State for Education at the time when concern about SATs was first expressed by teachers and parents. In your opinion, what would have been the best power strategy in these particular circumstances? Would you

   (a) hope to set the power groups in confrontation with each other in an attempt to divide and conquer?

    (b) avoid confrontation at all costs?

    (c) ignore the issue and hope it would go away?

    (d) look for some kind of compromise?

    (e) take a totally different course of action?

2. Now that you have selected your course of action you need to work out the best leadership strategies for achieving it. Make a few notes about what you would do.

3. How would this action affect teachers as
    (a) a power group?
    (b) as individuals in their classrooms?

4. If you have been working with other teachers or students share your notes with them. Within your group agree on the best possible course of action. How does this match your own individual plans? Is it an acceptable compromise or would you wish to contest it?

5. Why do you think teachers became so powerless in the SATs debate? What lessons can be learnt from this experience and what do you think teachers should do to prevent it from happening again in the future?

6. The SATs debate is only one example of an issue which affects teachers as a professional group and teachers as individuals in their classrooms. Make a note of any current issues which may be having similar effects. How would you describe the position of teachers in this particular power context? Is there anything that teachers could be doing to improve this situation?

10

Teaching and the negotiation of power

Taking a power perspective of the various duties which teachers perform helps us to understand the complexities of the teacher's work. Perhaps one of the most important points to have arisen is the fact that we cannot understand what teachers do in their classrooms unless we also look at the context in which teachers carry out their professional activities. The context in which teachers work is complex and structured by other power groups in the wider power context. Teachers are themselves a power group in this wider power context and their work is influenced by other power groups. The most powerful power group in society, for example, the government, produces legislation about what will be taught, how it will be monitored and what will happen to the results of the monitoring. Other power groups which influence the professional activities of teachers are 'the educational establishment', which might include some form of inspectorate, universities and research foundations producing research relevant to the activities of teachers and teacher training institutions. Further groups might include the judicial system, the medical service, the Church and the media.

The professional activities of teachers are also structured by power groups in the local community in which the school is situated. Perhaps the greatest influence here is that of parents, whose values and ideas are not only transmitted and brought into the school with the children but who also may have a more direct influence on what happens in a school as governors, assistants and helpers. Other local influences include local authorities, inspectors and advisers, academic advisory councils, the headteacher, the general ethos of the school and community.

Within the classroom the context of a teacher's professional activities is structured by the power relationships in the school by and with other teachers. It is also structured by the power relationships in the classroom, the knowledge which the teacher must teach and concrete limitations such as resources, building designs and the number of children in the class, which determine how the teacher will organise his or her work.

Some of the points emphasised by a power perspective are as follows:

- It is essential that teachers understand the power context of their work.
- It is essential that teachers are able to recognise and assess the power interests which structure the context of their work.
- It is essential that teachers have the ability to work within and to renegotiate the power constraints of their teaching context if they are to maintain their professional credibility in the wider power context and defend their right to professional practice.

Neverthless, it is important to remember that power is a two-way process. Just as the needs of the children affect what the teacher is likely to do in the classroom, so the teacher affects what can be achieved by his or her pupils. Just as the activities of the teacher are influenced by the local community and the wider power situation, so the activities of the teacher in turn influence the local community and, eventually, the wider power context. The classroom, the school, the local community and the wider national situation are all part of the same complex network of power interests and this is illustrated by the SATs debate.

In the SATs debate for example, we saw how the outcry from parents and teachers threatened the credibility of the government in an election year so that even the most powerful power group in society is not completely unassailable. From this example we saw how the power context, whether in the wider society or in the classroom of an individual teacher, is a two-way process which operated by a delicate balance of domination and consent. The power context of the classroom, the local community and the wider society are inextricably linked in a complex tapestry of power relationships. This is the professional context in which a teacher works.

In the course of this book we have examined the diverse activities which constitute a teacher's professional activities. In order to perform in these diverse ways teachers need to have a wide variety of skills, knowledge and understanding. But perhaps the most important of these skills are as follows:

- A teacher operates leadership in a power situation.
- The leadership skills of the teacher establish and maintain a

power situation which operates by consent and co-operation, which is not open to challenge and which allows the learning to proceed smoothly.
- The leadership skills of the teacher are to institute the most effective power strategies with individuals to maintain the balance of the power context.

In various examples throughout this book we have seen how teachers continually assess, work within and renegotiate the power relationships in their classrooms. They manipulate the power relationships and structure the future actions of their pupils in order to get their work done. Teachers' leadership skills not only require an understanding of the power context in which they work but also

- teachers leadership skills require them to have a knowledge of the variety of power strategies and power outcomes which will enable them to achieve their goals;
- power strategies are the means by which the teacher controls the learning experiences of the children in the classroom;
- power strategies enable teachers to create new learning opportunities for their pupils in the classroom.

The professional skill of the teacher is to operate within the effective limits of dominant and less dominant power strategies:

- An effective teacher uses dominant power strategies sparingly because they may lead to or heighten confrontations. Confrontations are situations which are open to challenge.
- An effective teacher relies heavily on less dominant power strategies because they are less open to challenge and secure consent over longer periods of time.
- An effective teacher is one who produces an acceptable balance between dominant and less dominant power strategies.

However, the situation for teachers is complicated by the context in which they work. In performing acts of leadership, a teacher does not simply circumscribe the actions of an individual child, or even a small group of children, as a parent might. Teachers circumscribe the possibilities for the future actions of thirty children simultaneously and they do this continuously throughout the day.

In order to do this, a teacher has to be a fast, clear and decisive thinker. The teacher has to have the ability to sum up situations in an instant and has to know what alternatives are open to him or her in the classroom. The teacher has to know how to structure the situation to achieve those alternatives. The strategies through which teachers accomplish their goals are communicated largely through language. Therefore in order to carry out their professional activities it is essential that teachers possess expert communication skills which far exceed the demands of everyday communication. In addition, when teachers address their classes, they use communication skills and strategies which are not required in the course of day-to-day communication.

These are some of the skills which make classroom teaching different from any other kind of teaching that other interested adults, such as parents, may perform. The ability to organise, manipulate, control and create new learning opportunities for thirty children simultaneously is the special professional skill which teachers, rather than any other group in society, are professionally equipped to perform.

Power is an important concept for classroom practice because it helps us to understand how the teacher manages the the classroom and why it is managed in particular ways. The important points to bear in mind when we look at what a teacher does from a power perspective are that power

- is a two-way process which operates a delicate balance between domination and consent;
- helps us to understand something about the teaching styles of different teachers. It is acted out in terms of habitually dominant or less dominant power strategies;
- gives us insights into the choices available to teachers in the classroom; and
- helps us to understand the professional skills of teachers.

Effective teachers have choices about how they manage the power relationships in their classrooms. We have seen how teacher identity and power strategies are inextricably linked. The kind of identity the teacher adopts determines the kinds of power strategies that the teacher will use:

- A dominant teacher identity demands dominant power relationship.
- A less dominant teacher identity demands a less dominant power relationship.

Effective teachers may have choices about how they manage the power relationships in their classrooms but this choice is limited. If a teacher adopts power strategies which are not sufficiently dominant and a less dominant identity, he or she would simply lose control of the learning situation. However, conversely, if the teacher adopts power strategies which are very dominant and a very dominant identity, this will produce conflict and will equally cause the teacher to lose control of the learning situation.

Effective teachers understand the benefits to be gained by adopting both dominant and less dominant power strategies in appropriate situations. They also understand that there are limits beyond which they must not go if they do not wish to lose control of the learning situation. Power helps us to understand something of the teacher's professional skills:

- The teacher's professional skill involves the ability to know when the greatest effects can be achieved by adopting dominant or less dominant power strategies.
- The teacher's professional skill involves the ability to recognise the upper and lower limits of dominant and less dominant power relationships.
- The teacher's professional skill involves the ability to manage the power relationships to the greatest effect in the classroom.

But the teacher's professional skill does not stop here. When considering the work teachers perform with their colleagues beyond the classroom, it was suggested that the teacher's professional skill extends into far wider areas. When the teachers were holding their planning meeting, it became clear that teachers have to have the ability to synthesise a wide range of issues before they can make teaching plans.

These issues ranged from understanding the legal requirements of the National Curriculum to understanding and applying theory about children's learning and considering the practicalities of resources and organisation. The teacher's planning meeting also revealed that teachers

- have to be literate in the language of their profession in order to carry out their work;
- have to have the ability to share and formulate professional knowledge with their fellow professionals;
- have to be prepared to influence and be influenced by the professional beliefs and values of their colleagues; and
- have to have the ability to analyse, define and articulate the immediate power context of their work and the work of their fellow professionals.

For these reasons teachers

- have to be able to establish and maintain continually their professional credibility amongst their colleagues.

This is the importance of a power perspective on a teacher's work.

Suggested reading

If you are interested in the idea of a teacher as a conflict manager the following are easy reading and provide worthwhile practical insights:

Berlak, A. and Berlak, H. (1981) *The Dilemmas of Schooling: Teaching and Social Change*, Methuen, London.

Lampert, M. (1984) Teaching about Thinking and Thinking about Teaching, *The Journal of Curriculum Studies*, Vol. 16, pp. 1–18.

Lampert, M. (1985) How do Teachers Manage to Teach? Perspectives on Problems and Practice, *Harvard Educational Review*, Vol. 55, no. 2, pp. 178–194.

Sachs, J. and Smith, R. (1988) Constructing Teacher Culture, *British Journal of Sociology of Education*, Vol. 9, no. 4, pp. 423–36.

If you are interested in the idea of power and power strategies an easy read is:

Sultana, R. (1989) Transition Education, Student Contestation and the Production of Meaning: Possibilities and Limitations of Resistance Theories, *British Journal of Sociology of Education*, Vol. 10, no. 3, pp. 287–309.

For a more demanding read try:

Aronowitz, A. and Giroux, H. (1985) *Education Under Siege*, Routledge & Kegan Paul, London.

Bennett, A. T. (1983) Discourses of Power, the Dialectics of Understanding, the Power of Literacy, *Journal of Education*, Vol. 165, pp. 53–74.

Giroux, H. (1983) *Theory and Resistance in Education: A Pedagogy for the Opposition*, Heinemann, London.

Giroux, H. and McLaren, P. (1987) Teacher Education as a Counter Public Sphere, in T. Popkewitz (ed.) *Critical Studies in Teacher Education: Its Folklore, Theory and Practice*, Falmer Press, Lewes.

Sola, M. and Bennett, A. T. (1985) The Struggle for Voice: Narrative Literacy and Consciousness in an East Harlem School, *Journal of Education*, Vol. 167, pp. 88–110.

If you are interested in power relationships the following are an easy read:

Apple, M. W. and Weis, L. (1985) Ideology and Schooling: The Relationship between Class and Culture, *Education and Society*, Vol. 3, no. 1, pp. 45–63.

Blake, R. and Mouton, S. R. (1969) Power, People and Performance Reviews, in K. Davis, and W. G. Scott, (eds.) *Human Relations and Organizational Behavior*, McGraw-Hill, New York.

For a more demanding read try:

Sholle, D. J. (1988) Critical Studies. From the Theory of Ideology to Power Knowledge, *Critical Studies in Mass Communication*, Vol. 5, Part 1, pp. 16–41.

For a very demanding read try:

Bennett, A. T. (1983) Discourses of Power, the Dialectics of Understanding, the Power of Literacy, *Journal of Education*, Vol. 165, pp. 53–74.

Cousins, M. and Hussain, A. (1984) *Michel Foucault*, Macmillan Education, London.

Foucault, M. (1982) The Subject and Power, *Critical Inquiry*, Vol. 8, Summer, pp. 777–95.

Frow, J. (1985) Discourse and Power, *Economy and Society*, Vol. 14, no. 2, pp. 193–214.

Therborn, G. (1980) *The Ideology of Power and the Power of Ideology*, Verso Editions and NLB, London.

Wickham, G. (1983) Power and Power Analysis beyond Foucault?, *Economy and Society*, Vol. 12, no. 4, pp. 470–98.

If you are interested in discourse structure, good introductory reads are:

Brazil, D., Coulthard, M. and Johns, C. (1980) *Discourse Intonation and Language Teaching*, Longman, London.

Brown, R. W. and Ford, M. (1964) Address in American English, in D. Hymes, (ed.) *Language in Culture and Society*, Harper International, New York.

Coulthard, M. (1977) *Introduction to Discourse Analysis*, Longman, London.

Sinclair, J. McH. and Coulthard, M. (1975) Towards an Analysis of Discourse: the English of Teachers and Pupils, Oxford University Press.

For a more advanced read try the following:

Hoey, M. (1979) *Signalling in Discourse*, Discourse Analysis Monographs, English Language Research, Birmingham University.

Sacks, H., Schegloff, E. A. and Jefferson, G. (1974) Simplest Systematics for the Organisation of Turn Taking in Conversation, *Language*, Vol. 50, no. 4, pp. 696–735.

If you are interested in the use of the voice for control in discourse try:

Brazil, D. (1975) *Discourse Intonation*, Monograph no.1, English Language Research, Birmingham.

If you are interested in the relationship between power and the professions, try:

Atkinson, P. and Delamont, S. (1990) *Professions and Powerlessness: Female Marginality in the Learned Occupations*, Routledge, London.

Johnson, T. (1972) *Professions and Power*, Macmillan, London.

Murray, T., Dingwall, R. and Eekelaar, J. (1983) Professionals in Bureaucracies, in R. Dingwall, and P. Lewis, (eds.) *Sociology of the Professions*, Macmillan, London.

Perkin, H. (1983) The Teaching Profession and the Game of Life, in P. Gordon, H. Perkin, H. Sockett, and E. Hoyle, (eds.) *Is Teaching a Profession?*, Bedford Way Papers, no. 15, Institute of Education, London.

If you are interested in the nature of professionalism, for an easy read try:

Blackington, F. H. and Patterson, R. (1968) *School, Society and the Professional Educator*, Holt, Rinehart & Winston, New York.

Hoyle, E. (1983) The Professionalisation of Teachers: A Paradox, in P. Gordon, H. Perkin, H. Sockett, and E. Hoyle (eds.) *Is Teaching a Profession?*, Bedford Way Papers, no. 15, Institute of Education, London.

Jarvis, P. (1983) *Professional Education*, Croom Helm, Beckenham.

Lieberman, M. (1956) *Education as a Profession*, Prentice-Hall, Engelwood Cliffs, NJ.

References

Bennett, A. T. (1983) Discourses of Power, the Dialectics of Understanding, the Power of Literacy, *Journal of Education*, Vol. 165, pp. 53–74.

Brazil, D. (1978) *Discourse Intonation 2*, Monograph no.2, English Language Research, Birmingham.

Foucault, M. (1982) The Subject and Power, *Critical Inquiry*, Vol. 8, Summer, pp. 777–95.

Hoey, M. (1979) *Signalling in Discourse*, Discourse Analysis Monographs, English Language Research, Birmingham University.

Lampert, M. (1985) How do Teachers Manage to Teach? Perspectives on Problems and Practice, *Harvard Educational Review*, Vol. 55, no. 2, pp. 178–94.

Sinclair, J. McH. and Coulthard, M. (1975) Towards an Analysis of Discourse: the English of Teachers and Pupils, Oxford University Press.

Sola, M. and Bennett, A. T. (1985) The Struggle for Voice: Narrative Literacy and Consciousness in an East Harlem School, *Journal of Education*, Vol. 167, pp. 88–110.

Index

adviser 62
aims 2, 62, 65–66, 82
approval 35

challenge 35, 53–55, 69–74, 78–90
co-operation 28–30, 58, 72–74, 90
community 88
competition 35–37, 80
compromise 3, 81–85, 87
conflict 2, 3, 53
conflict management 3
confrontation 21–22, 32–37, 80–82, 86, 90
consensus 53, 58
consent 53–58, 60–67, 72–75, 90–91
credibility 81, 89

dependent 33, 37
deputy head 62
discourse 21–24, 41–47, 68–69, 70
discourse sequence 11, 13, 22
discourse structure 11, 14, 24, 31
discussion 23–24, 31–35, 50–55, 69–75
disruption 21, 25, 36, 43, 78, 80
dominant identity 4, 6–7, 28, 80
dominant position 32, 61
dominant power relationship 91
dominant power strategies 9, 17, 21–27, 32–37
dominant rising tone 5, 7, 22, 47

encouragement 10, 34
equality 2, 35, 37
esteem 53
evaluation 7, 11–13, 68–70
exchange structure 12
external influences 62, 75

external pressures 73
eye contact 19, 21, 27, 34

facilitate 14
formal 56, 82

group relationship 59, 71

headteacher 62, 81, 88
hold the floor 5, 10–13, 14, 74
humour 20, 27, 46, 59

identity 10, 26–28, 34–37, 67
in-service 62
individual relationships 37
inequality 36
informal 56–57
inhibit 23–24, 47, 69, 70
interpersonal relationship 2, 51

justice 35

knowledge 9, 50–52, 89

leader 33, 61, 72–73
leadership 59, 61, 71–74, 81–83
learning context 28
less dominant identity 9, 13, 21, 57
less dominant power relationship 15, 20, 38, 73
less dominant power strategies 13–6, 34–37, 74, 90–92
limit 13, 37, 42–46, 81–92
literate 52, 54, 92

manage 4, 23, 37–39, 91–93

negotiate 30, 59, 90

opportunities 34, 42–47, 59,
    90–91
organisation 26, 34, 50–52, 92

parents 88–89, 91
personal relationship 72
planning 49–51, 62, 92
politeness 32, 70–74
power context 81, 84, 86, 88–89
power group 80–81, 84, 86, 88–89
power management 34, 84
power perspective 89, 91–92
power relationship 20–23, 32–39,
    88–89, 91–93
power situation 23–25, 71–74, 89
power strategy 32–33, 53–54, 67–71,
    86
power structure 25, 47, 68
praise 20, 21, 26, 42
professional activities 62, 88–89
professional attitude 52
professional context 89
professional credibility 53–55, 58,
    84–89, 92
professional issues 66
professional knowledge 54, 92
professional language 52, 54, 66
professional need 3

professional reasons 78–79
professional references 51, 54, 58
professional skills 38, 54, 58

quality of learning 28
questioning 23, 35, 50, 79

reading standards 62–63, 67–68, 74
relationship 37, 70, 76, 85
repetition 22, 42, 67–70
resources 41, 50, 89, 92
respect 35, 53
responsibility 12–13, 15, 31, 34
ritual 6, 41, 42
ritual language 5, 7, 41, 47
routine 5, 7, 16, 47

self-esteem 37
self-image 37
self-reliance 36
self-worth 36
state of play 11, 22–23, 47, 72
structure 22–24, 41–46, 67–69, 72–75
style 35, 36, 91
superior knowledge 24, 32–3, 35

teacher/pupil relationship 85
test 76–78, 81, 83, 85
topic 9, 13, 34, 49–51
trust 15, 35–36